Stitch by Stitch

Volume 3

TORSTAR BOOKS

NEW YORK · TORONTO

Stitch by Stitch

TORSTAR BOOKS INC.
300 E. 42ND STREET,
NEW YORK, NY 10017

Knitting and crochet abbreviations

approx = approximately	in = inch(es)	sl st = slip stitch
beg = begin(ning)	inc = increase(e)(ing)	sp = space(s)
ch = chain(s)	K = knit	st(s) = stitch(es)
cm = centimeter(s)	oz = ounce(s)	tbl = through back of
cont = continue(ing)	P = purl	loop(s)
dc = double crochet	patt = pattern	tog = together
dec = decreas(e)(ing)	psso = pass slipped	tr = triple crochet
dtr = double triple	stitch over	WS = wrong side
foll = follow(ing)	rem = remain(ing)	wyib = with yarn in
g = gram(s)	rep = repeat	back
grp = group(s)	RS = right side	wyif = with yarn in front
hdc = half double	sc = single crochet	yd = yard(s)
crochet	sl = slip	yo = yarn over

A guide to the pattern sizes

		10	12	14	16	18	20
Bust	in	32½	34	36	38	40	42
	cm	83	87	92	97	102	107
Waist	in	25	26½	28	30	32	34
	cm	64	67	71	76	81	87
Hips	in	34½	36	38	40	42	44
	cm	88	92	97	102	107	112

Torstar Books also offers a range of acrylic book stands, designed to keep instructional books such as *Stitch by Stitch* open, flat and upright while leaving the hands free for practical work.

For information write to Torstar Books Inc., 300 E.42nd Street, New York, NY 10017.

Library of Congress Cataloging in Publication Data
Main entry under title:

Stitch by stitch.

Includes index.
1. Needlework. I. Torstar Books (Firm)
TT705.S74 1984   746.4   84-111
ISBN 0-920269-00-1 (set)

9876543

© Marshall Cavendish Limited 1985

Printed in Belgium

ISBN 0-920269-03-6 (Volume 3)

Step-by-Step Crochet Course

Step-by-Step Knitting Course

Contents

Crochet / COURSE 11

*Increasing within a row
*Decreasing within a row
*Pattern for a chevron-striped skirt

Sometimes you will need to increase or decrease within a row, instead of at the ends, in order to produce the shape required. On a skirt, for example, the fabric must be shaped smoothly from the waist over the hips. Increasing or decreasing within the row achieves this. Another use for this kind of shaping is in making patterns, such as chevron stripes. By decreasing regularly at certain points you produce downward-pointing angles; by increasing regularly at intermediate points you produce upward-pointing angles, thus forming the familiar wave-like pattern.

Increasing within a row

Increasing within a row is very simple: you work two or more stitches into the stitch where the increase is required. It is a good idea to mark the stitch with a colored thread, since you will probably have to increase again on subsequent rows above it. Our sample is worked in doubles, but the technique is the same for other stitches.

1 Make 14 chains and work two rows in doubles. There will be 12 doubles in each row.

2 Work across the first four doubles of the next row: five doubles (counting the turning chain as one double).

3 Work two doubles into next stitch. Place a marker in the increased stitch.

4 Work one double into each double to end of row. Turn.

5 Work across the first five doubles of the next row: six doubles (counting the turning chain as one double).

6 Work two doubles into next stitch (the first of the two increased stitches).

7 Work one double into each double to end of row. Turn. Continue increasing in this way on the first of the increased stitches on the wrong side rows (this will be the second stitch on the right side rows). Note that the line of shaping produced in this way slants to the left on the right side of the fabric.

8 By increasing into the second of the two increased stitches on the wrong side (first of the increased stitches on the right side) you achieve a shaping that slants to the right. To keep the line of shaping vertical, increase the first of the increased stitches on every row.

Paul Williams

Decreasing within a row

The technique for decreasing within a row is essentially the same for each crochet stitch. Our sample is worked in doubles, but you can adapt the method for other stitches using the detailed directions for decreasing single crochet, half doubles or triples at the end of a row.

1 Make 14 chains and work two rows in doubles. There will be twelve doubles in each row.

2 Work across the first four doubles of the next wrong side row: five doubles (counting the turning chain as one double).

6 Repeat step 3 into the *next* stitch. Wind yarn around hook and draw through a loop. There should be four loops on the hook.

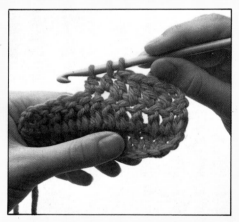

7 Repeat step 5. There will be three loops left on the hook this time.

8 Wind yarn around hook and draw through remaining three loops. One stitch has been decreased. Place a marker in the first stitch of the two you have worked together.

12 The line of decreases will slant to the left on the right side of the work.

13 To make the line of decreases slant to the right on the right side of the work, begin by repeating steps 1 to 9 as before.

14 Work across four doubles of next row; five doubles (counting the turning chain as one double).

3 Wind yarn around hook and insert hook into next stitch.

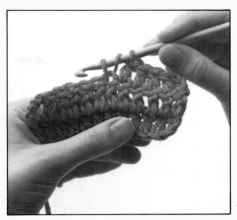

4 Wind yarn around hook and draw through a loop. There should be three loops on the hook.

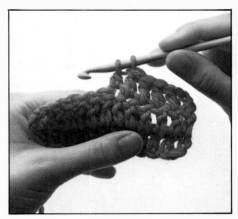

5 Wind yarn around hook and draw through first two loops on the hook. Two loops remain on the hook.

9 Work one double into each double to end of row. Turn.

10 Work across three doubles of next row: four doubles (counting the turning chain as one double).

11 Work the next two doubles together as for previous row.
Work one double into each double to the end of the row.

15 Work the next two doubles together as before.

16 Work one double into each double to end of row.

17 Here the line of decreases slants to the right. To keep the line of shaping vertical decrease to the right and to the left on alternate rows.

Paul Williams

Chevron skirt

Flattering chevron stripes in four shades of brown and beige make the shirt you see on page 4 a pleasure to wear. You'll also enjoy working the stripes and seeing their intriguing pattern emerge as you decrease the stitches.

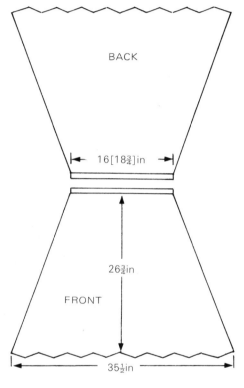

BACK

16[18¾]in

26¾in

FRONT

35½in

Sizes
To fit 36–38[40–42]in (91–97[102–107] cm) hips.
Length when hanging 26¾in (68cm).

Materials
Total of 16[22]oz (450[600]g) of a knitting worsted
This garment took 6[6]oz (150[150]g) in the first color, A
4[6]oz (100[150]g) in 2nd colour, B
4[6]oz (100[150]g) in 3rd color, C
4[6]oz (100[150]g) in 4th color, D
Size F (4.00mm) crochet hook
Waist length of 1in (2.5cm)-wide elastic; 7in (18cm) zipper

Gauge
15dc and 7½ rows to 4in (10cm) in plain dc; 17dc to 4in (10cm) in chevron.

Back and front (alike).
Using A, make 148[172]ch.
Base row 1dc into 4th ch from hook, *1dc into each of next 10ch, work 3dc together over next 3ch, 1dc into each of next 10ch, 3dc into next ch, repeat from asterisk (*) to end, but finish last repeat 2dc into last ch instead of 3dc. Turn. 145[169]dc.
Next row 3ch to count as 1dc, 1dc into first dc, *1dc into each of next 10dc, work 3dc together, 1dc into each of next 10dc, 3dc into next dc, repeat from * to end, but finish last repeat 2dc into turning ch of previous row and join B on last dc. Turn.
Repeat the last row, working 2 rows each in B, C, D, A, B, C and D and join A on last dc—so completing 16 rows from beginning.
1st decrease row Using A, work 3ch, skip first dc, 1dc into each of next 10dc, * work 3dc together, 1dc into each of next 21dc, repeat from * to end, but finish last repeat 1dc into each of last 1dc. Turn.
Next row 3ch, 1dc into first dc, * 1dc into each of next 9dc, work 3dc together, 1dc into each of next 9dc, 3dc into next dc, repeat from * to end, but finish last repeat 2dc into last dc, and join B on last dc. Turn. Using B, repeat the last row twice more, joining C on last dc of second row.
2nd decrease row Using C, work 3ch, 1dc into each of next 9dc, * work 3dc together, 1dc into each of next 19dc, repeat from * to end, but finish last repeat 1dc into each of last 10dc. Turn.
Next row 3ch, 1dc into first dc, * 1dc into each of next 8dc, work 3dc together, 1dc into each of next 8dc, 3dc into next dc, repeat from * to end, but finish last repeat 2dc into last dc, and join D on last dc. Turn.
Using D, repeat the last row twice more, joining A on last dc of second row.
3rd decrease row Using A, work 3ch, skip first dc, 1dc into each of next 8dc, * work 3dc together, 1dc into each of next 17dc, repeat from * to end, but finish last repeat 1dc into each of last 9dc. Turn.

Next row 3ch, 1dc into first dc, * 1dc into each of next 7dc, work 3dc together, 1dc into each of next 7dc, 3dc into next dc, repeat from * to end, but finish last repeat 2dc into last dc, and join B on last dc. Turn.
Continue in this way, working in stripe sequence and pattern as now set, decreasing on every 4th row, as before until 61[71]dc remain.
Work 7 rows, so ending 2 rows in D, joining A on last dc of 3rd row.
Next row Using A, work 1ch, skip first dc, * 1sc into next dc, 1hdc into each of next 2dc, 1dc into each of next 3dc, 1hdc into each of next 2dc, 1sc into next dc, repeat from * to end, finishing 1sc into last dc. Turn.
Work 4 rows in sc. Fasten off.

To finish
Do not block. Using a back stitch seam, join side seams leaving 7in (18cm) from top edge open. Sew in the zipper. Work catch-stitch casing over elastic on wrong side at waist. Press seams lightly according to type of yarn used.

Crochet / COURSE 12

*Making a flat square motif
*Introducing a new color
 in a square motif
*Sewing several motifs
 together
*Patterns for two multi-
 colored giant floor pillows

Making a flat square motif

Many different motifs can be produced by working in rounds to create a flat shape, but possibly the best known and easiest to work is the granny square. The squares can be worked in either one or several colors and joined together to make a great variety of rugs, blankets, shawls and garments.

To make this sample use a size G (4.5mm) hook and knitting worsted yarn.

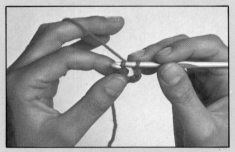

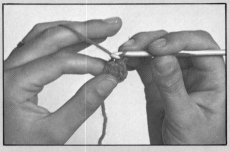

1 Make 8 chains and then loop the chain around to form a circle, inserting the hook from front to back into the first chain made.

2 Wind the yarn around the hook and draw it through both the loops on the hook, so that the chain is joined together with a slip stitch.

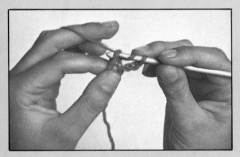

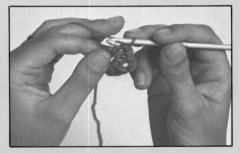

3 Work 3 chains which will count as the first double crochet of the first round. Now wind the yarn around the hook and insert the hook from front to back through the center of the circle—not into the chain stitch itself.

4 Complete this double in the normal way and then work one more double into the circle in the same way. There will now be one group of 3 doubles, including the first 3 chains, worked into the circle.

5 Make 2 chains. These 2 chains will be counted as the first corner of the square and will be called a 2-chain space. Now work 3 more doubles into the center of the circle as before.

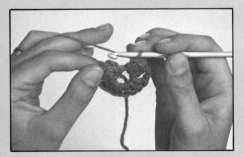

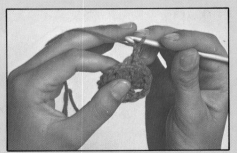

6 Repeat step 5 twice more, so that you have 4 groups of 3 doubles worked into the circle, and three 2-chain spaces. Work 2 chains for the last corner, and then insert the hook from front to back into the 3rd of the first 3 chains worked at the beginning of the round.

7 Wind the yarn around the hook and draw it through both loops on the hook so that the beginning and end of the round are joined together with a slip stitch. This completes the first round of the square.

8 Continue to work around the square, without turning the work, so that the right side of the motif is always facing you. Unlike working in rows, there is a definite right and wrong side to the fabric when working in rounds. Begin the 2nd round by working 2 chains.
continued

Fred Mancini

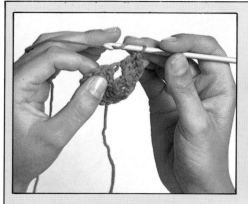

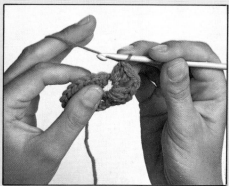

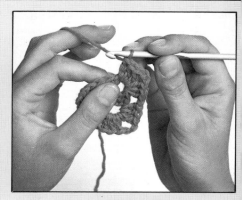

9 Work 3 doubles into the next 2-chain space after the first block of doubles worked in the first round, inserting the hook from front to back under the 2 chains each time.

10 Make 2 chains and then work 3 doubles into same space as the 3 doubles just worked. This will be the first corner group of the 2nd round. All the corners will be made this way on each round.

11 Make 1 chain and then work the next corner group as before into the next 2-chain space.

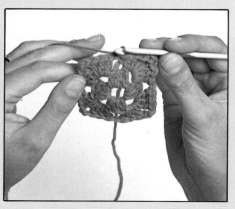

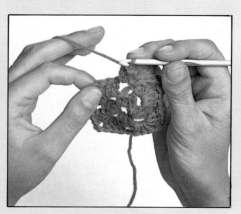

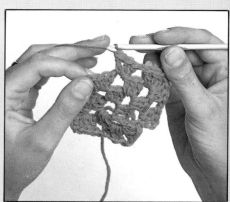

12 Complete the 3rd and 4th corners of the 2nd round in the same way. You will have now worked 4 corners in all with a 1-chain space between each corner. Join the end of the round to the beginning by working a slip stitch into the first of the 2 chains at the beginning of the round. The 2nd round has now been completed.

13 Work 3 chains to count as the first double of the next round. Now work 2 doubles into the first space after the slip stitch joining the previous round.

14 Work 1 chain and then work a corner group into the first corner space. Then work 1 chain, 1 group of 3 doubles into the 1 chain space on the previous row, then 1 chain.

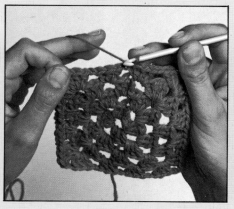

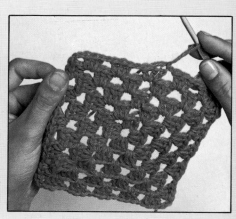

15 Complete the 3rd round in the same way, joining the last chain to the 3rd of the first 3 chains at the beginning of the round with a slip stitch.

16 The 4th round is worked in the same way, but with 2 groups of doubles worked in each of the 1-chain spaces on each side of the square.

17 To make the sample bigger, continue to work as many rounds as you like for the size of motif required, working 1 more doubles group on each side of the square on every subsequent round, with 1 chain between each group.

Introducing a new color in a square motif

Follow this method if you want to introduce a new color into the work without its showing in the previous round.

1 Complete the first round with the first color. When you have worked the final slip stitch joining the beginning and the end of the round, draw the yarn through the last loop and fasten off. Cut off the yarn, leaving a length long enough to be darned into the back of the fabric when the motif has been completed.

2 Insert the hook into the center of the next corner after the slip stitch that joined the ends of the last round together, and draw through a loop of the new color. Remember to leave a length of yarn long enough to be darned in afterward.

3 Work 1 chain with both ends of the yarn to hold it firmly in place. Now drop the free end of the yarn.

4 Work 2 more chains so that you have worked 3 chains in all, to count as the first double of this round. Complete the round in the normal way with the new color.

5 Change color at the beginning of each round in the same way until the motif has been completed.

6 Darn in all the loose ends on the back of the fabric, taking care to sew each end into its own color.

Sewing several motifs together

Use this method of joining motifs, such as granny squares, that have straight edges.

1 Place two motifs together, right sides together, so that the wrong side of each motif is on the outside. Pin them together along one side, about 1 round in from the edge.

2 For sewing the motifs together use a blunt-ended yarn needle and the yarn used in the motif. If this is too thick, use a matching yarn in a finer ply. Begin at the right-hand edge of the square and overcast the two together, taking care not to pull the yarn too tight.

3 Sew all the motifs together in the same way, sewing them first into horizontal strips and then sewing the strips together. By using this method, you will find it easier to get the seams to run straight.

Fred Mancini

Giant pillows

These floor pillows are almost a substitute for chairs. Make striking covers in bright-colored stripes, or use more natural shades for a pleasing subdued effect.

Multi-striped pillow

Size
Our cover has been made to fit a pillow form measuring 36 x 36in (91.5 x 91.5 cm). It measures approximately 35 x 35in (89 x 89cm), 1in (2.5cm) less than the form. Each square measures approximately 16½ x 16½in (42 x 42cm), excluding edging.

Materials
45oz (1250g) of a knitting worsted in blue
9oz (250g) in white
8oz (200g) each in red, green and yellow
Size F (4.00mm) crochet hook
A pillow form 36 x 36in (91.5 x 91.5cm)

Gauge
18hdc and 11 rows to 4in (10cm) on a Size F (4.00mm) hook.

Note To make the cover a different size, measure your pillow and make your cover 1in (2.5cm) smaller. This ensures a smooth, snug fit. For example, a pillow measuring 25 x 25in (63.5 x 63.5cm) will need a cover measuring 24 x 24in (61 x 61cm). Allow 1in (2.5cm) all around for edging and subtract this figure from the original size so that the area for remaining squares will be 22 x 22in (56 x 56cm). Each square will therefore measure approximately 11 x 11in (28 x 28cm).

To make the striped square
We quote the colors used in our pillow cover. You may, of course, use any color combination you like, but remember that you will need more of one color than the others to make the back.
Using size F (4.00mm) hook and red, ch10, join with a slip stitch to first ch to form a circle.
1st round Ch 2 to count as first hdc, then work 15hdc into circle; join the last hdc to the top of first 2ch worked with a slip stitch. There are 16hdc.
2nd round Ch2, which will count as first hdc; work 2hdc into same place as slip stitch—1 corner formed—, * 1hdc into each of next 3hdc, 3hdc all into next hdc —corner formed—, repeat from asterisk (*) twice more, then work 1hdc into each of next 3hdc, join last hdc worked

to top of first 2ch with a slip stitch. Fasten off.
3rd round Join white to 2nd hdc of one corner group, ch2, now work 1hdc, 1ch and 2hdc all into same hdc, *(1ch, skip next hdc, 1hdc into next hdc); work the section in parentheses () twice; 1ch, skip next hdc, work 2hdc, 1ch and 2hdc all into 2nd hdc of next corner group, repeat from * twice more (1ch, skip next hdc, 1hdc into next hdc) twice, 1ch, join last ch worked to 2nd of first 2ch. You should have three 1ch spaces between each corner group.
4th round Using white, slip stitch over first 2hdc and into the 1ch space at corner, 2ch, work 1hdc, 1ch and 2hdc all into same space, *1hdc into each of next 2hdc, (1hdc into next 1ch space, 1hdc into next hdc) 3 times, 1hdc into next hdc, 2hdc, 1ch and 2hdc all into 1ch space at corner, repeat from * to the end of the round, but do not work the last corner group at the end of the last repeat, join the last hdc worked to the 2nd of the first 2ch with a slip stitch. Fasten off. You should have worked 9hdc between each corner group.
5th round Join blue to 1ch space at one corner, 2ch, now work 1hdc, 1ch and 2hdc all into same space, *(1ch, skip next hdc, 1hdc into next hdc) to within 2nd hdc of next corner group, 1ch, skip next hdc, now work 2hdc, 1ch and 2hdc all into 1ch space at corner, repeat from * all around, but do not work the last corner group at the end of the last repeat; join the last ch worked to the 2nd of the first 2ch with a slip stitch. 7 spaces between each corner group.
6th round Using blue, slip stitch over first 2hdc and into the 1ch space at corner, 2ch, work 1hdc, 1ch and 2hdc all into same space, *1hdc into each of next 2hdc, (1hdc into next 1ch space, 1hdc into next hdc) to within 2nd hdc of next corner group, 1hdc into next hdc, 2hdc, 1ch and 2hdc all into 1ch space at corner, repeat from * to the end of the round, but do not work the last corner group at the end of the last repeat, join the last hdc worked to the 2nd of the first 2ch with a slip stitch. Fasten off. There should be 17hdc on each side between corner groups.
Continue to work the 5th and 6th rounds alternately working in a color sequence of 2 rounds yellow, 2 rounds green, 2 rounds red, 2 rounds white and

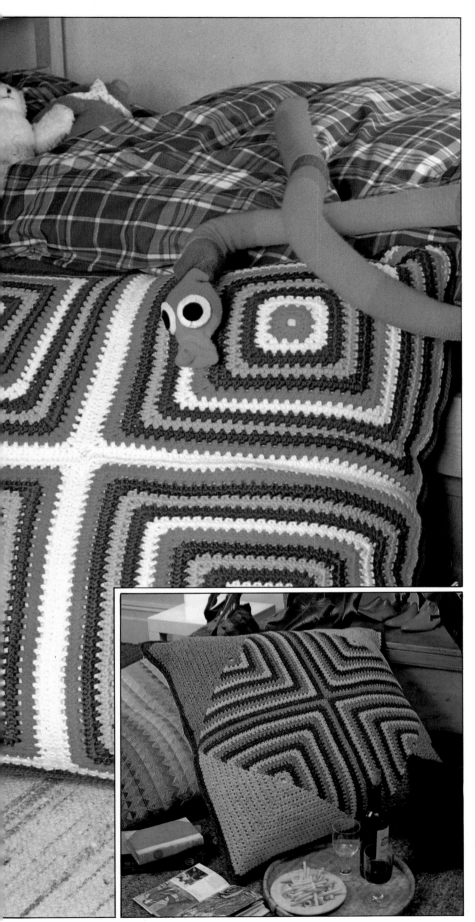

2 rounds blue until the 2nd round of the 3rd white stripe has been worked. Fasten off. This completes one square. Work 3 more squares in the same way.

To make the solid-color square
Using blue throughout, work the first circle and first and 2nd rounds as given for striped square.

3rd round Slip stitch into top of 2nd hdc of 3hdc at corner, work 2ch which will count as first hdc, now work 1hdc, 1ch and 2hdc all into same hdc for corner group, *(1ch, skip next hdc, 1hdc into next hdc) twice, 1ch, skip next hdc, work 2hdc, 1ch and 2hdc all into 2nd hdc of next corner group, repeat from * twice more, (1ch, skip next hdc, 1hdc into next hdc) twice, 1ch, join last ch to 2nd of first 2ch worked.
There will be three 1ch spaces between each corner group.

4th round Slip stitch over first 2hdc and into the 1ch space at corner, 2ch, work 1hdc, 1ch and 2hdc all into same space, *1hdc into each of next 2hdc, (1hdc into next 1ch space, 1hdc into next hdc) 3 times, 1hdc into next hdc, 2hdc, 1ch and 2hdc all into 1ch space at corner, repeat from * to the end of the round, but do not work the last corner group at the end of the last repeat, join the last hdc worked to the 2nd of the first 2ch with a slip stitch.

5th round Slip stitch over first 2hdc and into the 1ch space at corner, 2ch, now work 1hdc, 1ch and 2hdc all into same space, *(1ch, skip next hdc, 1hdc into next hdc) to within 2nd hdc of next corner group, 1ch, skip next hdc, now work 2hdc, 1ch and 2hdc all into 1ch space at corner, repeat from * all around but do not work the last corner group at the end of the last repeat, join the last ch worked to the 2nd of the first 2ch with a slip stitch.
Continue working rounds 4 and 5 until square measures the same as the striped square. Fasten off. Work three more squares in the same way.

To finish
Darn in all loose ends on the wrong side of each square, keeping each color in its own stripe.
With the right side of two striped squares together, using white yarn and a flat seam, join one edge of the squares together. Join the other two striped squares in the same way. Now join these two pieces to make one large square. Join the solid-color squares in the same way.

The edging
With the right side of one large square facing, insert hook into one corner space and draw a loop of blue through, ch2, work 1hdc, 1ch and 2hdc all into same space, *(1ch, skip next 1hdc, 1hdc into next hdc) along edge to corner, 1ch, skip

next hdc, work 2hdc, 1 ch and 2hdc all into corner space, repeat from * all around, but do not work corner group at end of last repeat, join last 1 ch worked to 2nd of the first 2ch with a slip stitch.

Next round Work as given for 4th round of solid square. Fasten off.

Work around outer edge of other large square in the same way. Darn in all loose ends on wrong side of work.

To join large squares together

With wrong sides facing join blue; working through double thickness work a row of sc around 3 sides of cover, working 1sc into each hdc and 2sc into each space at corner. Fasten off. Insert pillow form, then join remaining seam. You could insert a zipper on this side.

Diagonally striped pillow

Sizes

Our cover has been made to fit a pillow form 36 x 36in (91.5 x 91.5cm). The cover measures approximately 35 x 35in (89 x 89cm) — 1in (2.5cm) smaller than form. Each square measures 16½ x 16½in (42 x 42cm), excluding edging.

Materials

50oz (1400g) of a knitting worsted in dark brown, A
20oz (550g) each of beige, B, and gray, C
Size F (4.00mm) crochet hook
A pillow form 36 x 36in (91.5 x 91.5cm)

Gauge

18hdc and 11 rows to 4in (10cm) worked on a Size F (4.00mm) hook.

Note If you wish to alter the size of the cover, measure the width of your pillow and make your cover 1in (2.5cm) less. For example a pillow measuring 25in (63.5cm) square will need a cover measuring 24in (61cm) square. Allow 1in (2.5cm) all around for edging subtracting this figure from the total size so that the area remaining for squares will be 22 x 22in (56 x 56cm). Each square will measure about 11 x 11in (28 x 28cm).

To make the striped square

Each square is worked in stripes on one half, with the other half being worked in one color only. Be careful when changing colors to avoid making a hole between the stitches.

Using Size F (4.00mm) hook and B, ch 10, join with a slip stitch to first ch to form a circle.

1st round Work 2ch, which will count as first hdc, then work 15hdc into the circle; join the last hdc to the 2nd of the

first 2ch worked with a slip stitch. There are 16hdc.

6th round Work 2ch, which will count as first hdc, then work 2hdc into the same place as slip stitch — 1 corner formed —, *work 1 hdc into each of the next 3hdc, 3hdc all into next hdc — corner formed —, repeat from asterisk (*) twice more, work 1 hdc into each of next 3hdc, join the last hdc worked to top of the first 2ch to complete the round. Begin striped pattern.

3rd round Using B, work 1 slip stitch into 2nd hdc of group at corner, 2ch, 1 hdc into same place as slip stitch, (1ch, skip next hdc, 1hdc into next hdc) work the section in parentheses ( ) twice; 1ch skip next hdc, now work 2hdc, 1ch and 2hdc all into 2nd hdc of next corner group, (1ch, skip next hdc, 1hdc into next hdc) twice, 1ch, skip next hdc, work 2hdc into 2nd hdc of the next corner group, join second color by drawing C through working loop. Cut off B. Complete the round in C by working 2hdc into same hdc as last 2hdc, (1ch, skip next hdc, 1hdc, into next hdc) twice, 1ch, skip next hdc, now work 2hdc, 1ch and 2hdc all into 2nd hdc of next corner group, (1ch, skip next hdc, work 1 hdc into next hdc) twice, 1ch, skip next hdc, work 2hdc into same hdc as first 2hdc, 1ch, insert hook into the 2nd of the first 2ch, and draw B through. Cut off C. There should be three 1ch spaces between each corner group.

4th round Using B, work 2ch, 1hdc into 1ch space at corner, 1hdc into each of next 2hdc, (1hdc into next 1ch space, 1 hdc into next hdc) 3 times, 1hdc into next hdc, now work 2hdc, 1ch and 2hdc all into corner space, 1hdc into each of next 2hdc, (1hdc into next 1ch space, 1 hdc into next hdc) 3 times, 1hdc into next hdc, 2hdc into 1ch space at corner. Join second color by drawing C through working loop. Cut off B. Complete round in C by working 2hdc into same place as last 2hdc, 1hdc into each of next 2hdc, (1hdc into next space, 1hdc into next hdc) 3 times, 1hdc into next hdc, now work 2hdc, 1ch and 2hdc all into next space at corner, 1hdc into each of next 2hdc, (1hdc into next 1ch space, 1hdc into next hdc) 3 times, 1hdc into next hdc, 2hdc into same spaces as first 2hdc, 1ch, insert hook into 2nd of first 2ch and draw B through. Cut off C.

5th round Work 2ch, 1hdc into 1ch space at corner, (1ch, skip next hdc, 1hdc into next hdc) to within 2nd hdc of corner group, 1ch, skip next hdc, now work 2hdc, 1ch and 2hdc all into 1ch space at corner, (1ch, skip next hdc, 1hdc into next hdc) to within 2nd hdc of next corner group, 1ch, 2hdc into 1ch space at corner. Join 2nd color by drawing A through working loop. Cut off B. Complete round in A, finishing by

working 2hdc into same space as first 2hdc, 1ch, insert hook into the 2nd of first 2ch and draw B through. Cut off A.

6th roung Work 2ch, 1hdc into 1ch space at corner, continue to work as for 4th round, working 1hdc into each hdc and 1ch space and 2hdc, 1ch and 2hdc all into 1ch space at corners. Remember to change from B to A at corner, as before. Continue to work stripes of 2 rounds in each color, keeping one half in B and working the other half in color sequence of C, A and B throughout. Make sure that the pattern is correct when changing colors at corners. As the square increases in size the length of each stripe will also be extended. Continue to work the square until it measures approximately 16½in (42cm) square. Fasten off.

Make one more square in the same way. Make two squares, keeping the stripe sequence the same but working the solid half in C instead of B. These 4 squares form the top of the pillow cover.

To make the solid squares

Using A only throughout, work 4 squares as given for solid-color square on multi-striped cover.

To finish

Darn in all loose ends to the wrong side of each square.

With the right sides of two striped squares together, using the corresponding color and a flat seam join one edge of the squares. Join the other two striped squares in the same way. Now join these 2 pieces together, matching the stripes, to make one larger square.

Join the plain squares in the same way.

The edging

With right side of large square facing, insert hook into one corner space and draw a loop of A through, 2ch, work 1hdc, 1ch and 2hdc all into same space, *(1ch, skip next hdc, 1hdc into next hdc) along edge to corner, 1ch, skip next hdc, work 2hdc, 1ch and 2hdc all into corner space, repeat from * all around but do not work corner group at end of last repeat, join last 1ch worked to 2nd of the first 2ch with a slip stitch.

Next round Work as given for 4th round of solid square. Fasten off. Work around outer edge of other square in the same way. Darn in loose ends on wrong side.

To join the squares together

With wrong sides facing, join A and, working through double thickness, work a row of sc around 3 sides of cover, working 1sc into each hdc and 2sc into each space at corner. Fasten off. Insert pillow form, then join the remaining seam in the same way. You could insert a zipper on this side.

Crochet / COURSE 13

More about motifs

Now that you have mastered the basic principles of working a square motif, try making this pretty square with the spiked wheel center. The center of the motif is worked in a circular shape with the corners and straight sides being added on the last two rounds — unlike the granny square, in which the four corners of the motif are made on the first round. Our motif has been worked in a sport yarn using a size E (3.50mm) hook. Try making the same motif in several colors or using different yarns and hook sizes to see the variety of effects you can achieve. A motif worked in a fine cotton will look very different from the same motif worked in a bulky yarn with a large hook.

1 Chain 8 and join in a circle with a slip stitch. Now work 2 chains to count as the first double crochet, followed by 15 doubles into the circle. Join the last double to the first 2 chains with a slip stitch. Join each round in the same way.

2 Chain 5 to count as the first double and 2 chain space of the next round. Now work 1 double followed by 2 chains into each stitch all around the circle. Join the last chain to the top of 3 chains at the beginning of round.

3 Chain 3 to count as the first double of the next round. Now work 2 doubles into the first 2 chain space. This will be the first block of doubles.

4 Chain 1, then work 3 doubles into the next 2 chain space.

5 Repeat step 4 all around the circle so that there are 16 blocks of doubles with 1 chain between each block. Join last chain to top of the first 3 chains.

6 Chain 3 and then work 1 single crochet into the next 1 chain space. Repeat this twice more so that there are 3 loops on this side of the circle.

7 Work the first corner of the square by making 6 chains and then working 1 single crochet into the next 1 chain space.

8 Repeat steps 6 and 7 all around the motif so that there are 3-chain loops on each side with a 6-chain loop at each corner, and 1 single crochet worked into each 1 chain space. Join last chain to base of first 3 chains.

9 Chain 3 to count as the first double of the next round and then work 2 doubles into the first 2 chain space.

continued

10 Now work 3 doubles into each of the next two 3-chain loops on the side of the square.

11 Work 5 doubles followed by 2 chains and 5 doubles all into the next 6-chain loop at the corner.

12 Continue to work around the square in the same way, with 3 blocks of 3 doubles on each side and 5 doubles, 2 chains and 5 doubles all into the 6-chain loop at each of remaining 3 corners. Join the last double to the top of the first 3 doubles. This completes the motif.

Working a picot edging

There are various picot edgings which can be worked with a crochet hook directly on the edge of the fabric, the simplest being that featured on the baby's cape in this course. As picot edgings are worked into the edge of the fabric, they can be used not only as a decorative trimming but also to finish an uneven edge or hem on a crocheted or knitted fabric. They can be worked in either rows or rounds in any thickness of yarn, from a fine cotton for a delicate trimming on table linens to a thick wool for a bulky cardigan or tunic. Our sample has been worked in a sport yarn on a single crochet fabric. Once you have mastered the technique, try using a fine hook and crochet cotton for a different effect.

1 With the right side of the work facing, make 5 chains at the right-hand edge of the fabric to count as the first half double and 2-chain space.

2 Skip the next 2 stitches and then work 1 half double into the next stitch.

3 Make 2 chains and then repeat step 2 once more.

4 Repeat step 3 all along the edge of the fabric, working the last half double into the turning chain at the end of the last row of the main fabric. You have now worked a series of 2-chain spaces with 1 half double between each space.

5 Turn. Work 1 single crochet into the first space, inserting the hook from front to back under the 2 chains worked in the previous row.

6 Make 3 chains and then work 1 slip stitch into the first of these 3 chains to form the picot point.

7 Work another single crochet into the same space, as before, so that 1 picot block has now been completed.

8 Continue to work 1 picot block in exactly the same way into each chain space to the end of the row to complete the edging.

Joining motifs with a slip stitch

Square motifs with straight side edges can be joined together with a slip stitch to make a very firm seam with a raised appearance. Use this method of seaming on a bulky rug or blanket to make sure that the motifs are joined firmly and to make a feature of the seams.

1 Hold the two motifs to be joined with the wrong sides together and insert the hook through both corners.

2 Draw a loop of yarn through both corners and make 1 chain to hold the yarn in place.

3 Work 1 slip stich into the next stitch, working through both thicknesses.

4 Continue to work 1 slip stitch into each stitch along the edge of the motifs, taking care to work into the corresponding stitch on each motif.

5 When laid flat the seams thus joined are raised, producing a kind of lattice effect.

Fred Mancini

Cozy hooded cape

What could be easier to make—or more comfortable for a baby to wear—than this pretty cape? The pastel random-dyed yarn gives a soft effect to the motifs, which are sewn together in a simple rectangular shape. The picot edging is worked after the hood and cape have been joined.

Sizes
To fit a baby up to 3 months old.
Length to shoulder, 19¼in (49cm)
Length of hood to shoulder, 8¼in (21cm)

Materials
*Total of 11oz (300g) of random-dyed
    knitting worsted in any desired baby
    colors*
Size C (3.00mm) crochet hook
Size E (3.50mm) crochet hook
1 button

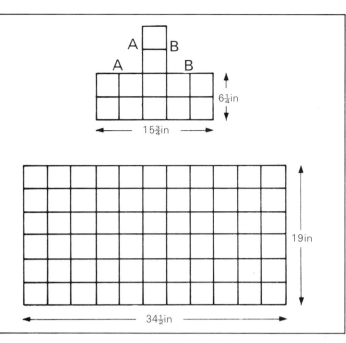

David Laraman

Serge Kroulikoff

Gauge
1 motif measures 3⅛in (8cm) square worked on a size E (3.50mm) hook.

The motif
Using size E (3.50mm) hook, make 6ch. join with a sl st to first ch to form a circle.
1st round 3ch to count as first dc, then work 19dc into the circle, join the last dc to the 3rd of the first 3ch with a sl st.
2nd round 1ch to count as first sc, 1hdc into next dc, work 1dc, 3ch and 1dc all into next dc—corner formed—, 1hdc into next dc, * 1sc into each of next 2dc, 1hdc into next dc, now work 1dc, 3ch and 2dc all into next dc—corner formed—, 1hdc into next dc, rep from * twice more, 1sc into next dc, join last sc to the first ch with a sl st.
3rd round 3ch, 1dc into each of next 2 sts, work 2dc, 3ch and 2dc all into loop at corner—called 1 grp * 1dc into each of next 6 sts, work 1 grp into center of loop at corner, rep from * twice more, 1dc into each of last 3 sts, join last dc to 3rd of first 3ch with a sl st.
4th round 3ch, 1dc into each of next 4dc, 1 grp into center of grp at corner, * 1dc into each of next 10dc, work 1 grp into center of grp at corner rep from * twice more, 1dc into each of next 5dc, join last dc to 3rd of first 3ch with a sl st. Fasten off.
Make 65 more motifs in same way for cape and then make 12 for hood.

Cape
Darn in all loose ends to wrong side of motifs. Overcast motifs together, placing them as shown in diagram.

Edging
With right side of work facing, join yarn to first corner of 2nd motif on one long side and using size E (3.50mm) hook work 1sc into this loop, * 1sc into each dc to next corner, 1sc into corner loop, then 1sc into corner loop of next motif, rep from * to end, working last sc into last corner loop. Turn.
Next row 1ch, (insert hook into next sc and draw a loop through) twice, yarn around hook and draw through all 3 loops on hook—one sc decreased; decrease 1sc in this way over every 2sc to end of row. Fasten off.

Hood
Darn in all loose ends to wrong side of motifs. Overcast motifs together placing them as shown in diagram, sewing seams A to A and B to B.

Edging
With right side of work facing, join yarn. Using size E (3.50mm) crochet hook work 1sc into each dc and loop along lower edge. Fasten off.

To join hood and cape
With right sides together join yarn to corner of first motif on cape and working through the double thickness join the lower edge of the hood to the top edge of the cape by working 1sc into each sc. Fasten off.

Edging
With right side of work facing, join yarn to lower edge at center back and using size C (3.00mm) hook work * 1sc into each dc and 1sc into each corner loop along lower edge to corner, work 3sc into the corner loop, rep from * to corner at neck edge, work 3sc into corner, continue to work in this way around hood and down other side of cape to center back; join with a sl st to first sc. Do not turn.
Next row 1ch, * 1sc into each of next 3sc, 3ch, sl st into top of last sc worked—1 picot formed; rep from * all around

edge of cape and hood, join with sl st to first ch. Fasten off.
Sew a button to left front, 1 motif in from left front neck edge, and use corner sp on first motif on right for buttonhole. Block according to yarn used, pressing lightly on the wrong side.

Ties
Using size E (3.50mm) hook and yarn double throughout make a ch 16½in (42cm) long. Fasten off.
Make another tie in the same way.
Sew 1 tie to each side of hood at neck.

Crochet / COURSE 14

Joining lace motifs with crochet

Once you have completed the first motif of a lacy fabric, you can join the second and all subsequent motifs while working the last round of each. Working in this way not only maintains the continuity of the lace pattern but also greatly enhances the motifs themselves.

The beautiful bedspreads and lace table-cloths characteristic of traditional crochet are frequently worked in this way. Crochet patterns usually give detailed directions on how to join the particular motifs you are working. They may appear complicated, but don't be put off.

If you follow the directions carefully you will get beautiful results.
The step-by-step directions given here are for joining two of the motifs used in the tablecloth featured in this course, but the principle is the same for any motif with lace edges.

1 Begin the sample by working the first motif from the tablecloth directions and the first 5 rounds of the second motif.

2 Hold the first motif behind the 2nd motif with the wrong sides of the squares together. Match 1 corner picot of the first motif to the working loop at the end of the 5th round on the 2nd motif.

3 Work 1 single crochet through the corner picot of the first motif to join the squares together. The single crochet will count as the corner picot of the 2nd motif.

4 Leave the first motif. Make 2 chains and then work 3 doubles into each of the next 3 doubles on the 2nd motif, thus continuing to work the 6th round of the 2nd motif.

5 Hold the 2 motifs together again, matching the block of 3 doubles just worked with the corresponding 3 doubles on the first motif. Work 1 slip stitch into the first chain of the next 5 chain loop on the first motif.

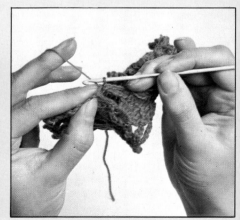

6 Leave the first motif. Work 4 chains and then 1 slip stitch into the next single crochet on the second motif.

7 Work 1 chain, hold the 2 motifs together as before and work 1 single crochet into the next 4 chain picot on the first motif.

8 Leave the first motif and work 1 chain. Skip the next single crochet on the 2nd motif and then work 1 slip stitch into the next single crochet of the same motif.

9 Work 4 chains. Hold the 2 motifs together and then work 1 slip stitch into the last chain before the next block of 3 doubles on the first motif.

10 Leave the first motif. Work 1 double into each of the next 3 doubles on the 2nd motif. Work 2 chains. Hold the 2 motifs together and work 1 single crochet into the centre of the picot on the next corner of the first motif. One side of each square has now been joined.

11 Complete the 6th round of the 2nd motif in the same way as given for the second motif of the tablecloth. Join the last stitch to the first with a slip stitch.

12 Where the motifs are being joined in strips, each consecutive motif should be joined in the same way. Remember to work the first 5 rounds of the 2nd motif each time.

Joining lace motifs to make a square fabric

When two sides of a motif are to be joined to produce a square fabric, the working method is exactly the same as for joining them in a strip, but it is important to work the joins in the crochet order, so that the motifs are crocheted together evenly. The step-by-step directions that follow here relate to the tablecloth pattern, but apply to other square fabrics as well.

1 After completing the first row, or strip, of motifs, work the first 5 rounds of the first motif of the second row. Join one side of this motif to the lower edge of the first motif of the first row. Complete the sixth round.

2 Work the first 5 rounds of the next motif. With the wrong side of both motifs facing, hold the first and second motifs of this row together so that the bottom left-hand corner of the first motif corresponds to the working loop on the second motif.

continued

3 Work 1 single crochet into the first corner picot of the first motif. This single crochet will count as the first corner picot of the 6th round on the second motif.

4 Join the 2 motifs on this side in same way as before, making sure you work the last single crochet on this side into the center of the corner where the first 3 motifs meet. You will be working the 6th round of the 2nd motif at the same time as joining the 2 motifs.

5 Turn the work so that the first row of motifs is at the top of your work and the first motif of the 2nd row on the right-hand side.

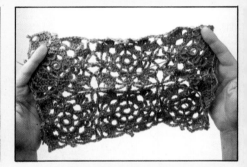

6 Now join the top of the 2nd motif of the 2nd row to the bottom of the 2nd motif of the first row in the same way as before, beginning by working 2 chains and then 3 doubles into the first 3 doubles on the 2nd motif.

7 Complete the 6th round of the 2nd motif, working around the remaining 2 sides of the square and joining the last stitch to the corner picot on the first motif.

8 Work subsequent joins in the same way, making sure that you always work from the bottom left-hand corner of the motif to the right of the one to be joined, then up and across to the top left-hand corner of the motif being joined. In this way each motif will be joined correctly to the one before.

Joining simple squares with lace crochet

Square motifs with straight sides can also be joined with crochet by working a picot or decorative edging around the first square and then using the same edging to join the following motifs together. Once you have mastered the basic technique you will be able to join any square in the same way, using a variety of picot edgings. This will enable you to combine a motif and edging of your choice and create your own fabric.

The edging you use will depend on the size of motif you wish to make and the type of yarn being used. To follow these step-by-step directions, first make 2 granny squares (Crochet course 12, page 9). Work only 3 rounds for each motif.

1 With the right side of one motif facing, join the yarn to any corner space and make 4 chains. Work 1 single crochet into the 3rd chain from the hook to form a picot point. Now work 1 single crochet into the same corner space. This space will now be referred to as a 4-chain corner picot.

2 Work 1 single crochet into the next double, then 4 chains and then 1 single crochet into the following double. This makes one 4-chain loop.

3 Work 4 chains and then 1 single crochet into the next chain loop on the previous round, making the 2nd 4-chain loop on the side of the square.

4 Repeat steps 2 and 3 and then step 2 once again. There will now be 5 loops on this side of the square.

5 Work 1 single crochet into the chain loop of the previous round at the next corner. Now work a 4-chain corner picot into the same loop.

6 Continue to work all around the square in the same way, making 5 loops on each side and one 4-chain corner loop on each corner. Join the last single crochet to the first chain worked at the beginning of the round. This completes the decorative edging for the first motif.

7 With the right side of the 2nd motif facing, join the yarn to any corner space and work 2 chains. Hold the first and 2nd motifs together with the wrong sides together, and work a slip stitch into the top of the picot point at one corner on the first motif.

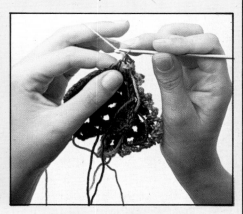

8 Work 2 chains and then 1 single crochet into the same space on the 2nd motif to complete the corner on the 2nd motif.

9 Work 1 single crochet into the next stitch on the 2nd motif, then 2 chains. Hold the motifs together and work a slip stitch into the top of the first loop on the first motif, working through the stitch rather than under the loop.

10 Work 2 chains and then 1 single crochet into the next double on the 2nd motif. Now work 2 chains then 1 slip stitch into the top of the next loop on the first motif.

11 Work 2 chains and then 1 single crochet into the next chain loop on the 2nd motif.

continued

12 Repeat steps 9 to 11. Now work 1 single crochet into the next stitch.

13 Work 2 chains and then 1 slip stitch into the last loop on the side of the first motif. Now work 2 chains and 1 single crochet into the next stitch on the 2nd motif. Work one more single crochet into the next corner space on the 2nd motif and join it to the picot on the first motif as before, thus joining the two sides together.

14 Complete the picot edging around the remaining 3 sides of the 2nd square in the same way as given for the first motif. When joining the motifs on 2 sides, remember to start at the bottom left-hand corner of the motif to the right of the one being joined, then up and across to the top left-hand corner of the motif being joined.

Lacy tablecloth

Small motifs worked in a fine thread and crocheted together in strips make a lovely tablecloth, equally suitable for a round or square table. Lay it over a plain cloth in a contrasting color to show off its delicate texture.

Size
$30\frac{1}{4}$in (.77m) at the widest part.

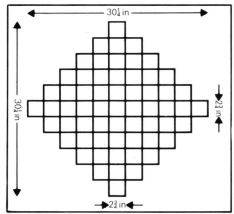

Materials
Total of 732yd (150g) of medium-weight mercerized crochet cotton
Steel crochet hook No. 0 (2.00mm)

Gauge
1 motif measures $2\frac{3}{4}$in (7cm) square on steel hook No. 0 (2.00mm).

First motif
6ch, join with a sl st to first ch to form circle.
1st round 2ch to count as first sc, work 15sc into circle, join with a sl st to second of first 2ch.
2nd round 4ch to count as first hdc and 2ch, * skip next sc, 1hdc into next sc, 2ch, rep from * 6 times more, join with a sl st to second of first 4ch.
3rd round Work * 1sc, 1hdc, 1dc, 1hdc and 1sc all into next ch sp, 1ch, rep from * to end, join with a sl st to first sc. 8 petals.
4th round 2ch to count as at corner of first * 3ch, 1sc into dc of sc of next petal, 4ch, 1sc into dc of next petal, 3ch, 1hdc into 1ch sp before next petal, 2ch, 1hdc into same ch sp, rep from * twice more, 3ch, 1sc into dc of next petal, 4ch, 1sc into dc of next petal, 3ch, 1hdc into last 1 ch sp after last petal, 2ch, join with sl st to second of first 2ch.
5th round 1ch, * 4ch, now work 3dc, 3ch and 3dc all into next 4ch sp to form corner, 4ch, 1sc into next hdc, 1sc into next 2ch sp, 1sc into next hdc, rep from * twice more, 4ch, now work 3dc, 3ch and 3dc all into next 4ch sp, 4ch, 1sc into next hdc, 1sc into next 2ch sp, join with a sl st to first ch.
6th round 1ch, *5ch, 1dc into each of next 3dc, 5ch, insert hook into 3rd ch from

hook to form a little loop and work 1sc to form picot—called 5ch picot—, 2ch, 1dc into each of next 3dc, 5ch, sl st into next sc, 4ch, insert hook into 3rd ch from hook and work 1sc to form picot—called 4ch picot—, 1ch, skip next sc, sl st into next sc; rep from * twice more, 5ch 1sc into each of next 3dc, work a 5ch picot, 2ch, 1 dc into each of next 3dc, 5ch sl st into next sc, work a 4ch picot, 1ch, join with a sl st to first ch. Fasten off.

Second motif
Work as given for first motif to end of round 5.
6th round (joining round) 1ch, *5ch, 1dc into each of next 3dc, 2ch, with right side

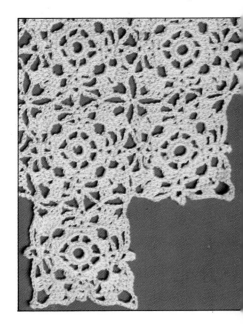

of completed motif facing right side of second motif, which is to be joined, work 1sc into 5ch picot at corner of first motif, 2ch, 1dc into each of next 3dc of second motif, sl st into first 5ch after last dc on first motif, 4ch, sl st into next sc of second motif, 1ch, 1sc into 4ch picot of first motif, 1ch, skip next sc on second motif, sl st into next sc on second motif, 4ch, sl st into last ch before next 3dc on first motif, 1dc into each of next 3dc on second motif, 2ch, 1sc into 5ch picot at corner of first motif, 2ch. One side has been joined. Complete motif as given for first motif. Fasten off.

Make a strip of 11 joined motifs. Make and join 50 more motifs, placing them as shown in diagram. When two sides have to be joined, join the first side to the preceding motif on the same strip and the second side to the corresponding motif on the preceding strip. Block according to yarn used, pressing lightly.

*Working narrow horizontal
 stripes
*Horizontal stripes in garter
 and stockinette stitch
*Working narrow vertical
 stripes
*Joining shoulder seams
*Pattern for a baby's striped rob

Working narrow horizontal stripes

Narrow horizontal stripes are easy to work in a variety of knitted fabrics and are particularly popular in stockinette stitch and garter stitch. To avoid having to darn in loose ends, don't cut off the yarn, but carry it up the right-hand edge of the work and resume knitting with it where necessary. Be careful not to pull the yarn so tightly between stripes that it distorts the fabric and draws the rows together at the right-hand edge. This method works only if the stripes are close together — ¾–1½in (2–3cm) apart.

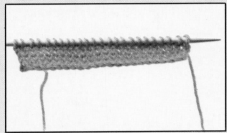

1 To make a regular striped stockinette-stitch fabric in 3 colors, cast on the required number of stitches with 1 of the colors. Work an even number of rows in stockinette stitch—here there are 4. Limit yourself to 3 or 4 colors of yarn, so you can carry the yarn up the side of the work loosely.

2 Without breaking off the first color, take a ball of the second color and begin knitting with it. The ends of yarn are at the right-hand (RH) edge.

3 Work 4 rows in stockinette stitch using the second color. Note the row of broken stripes immediately below the one you are working; this effect occurs on the wrong side of the fabric when you change color.

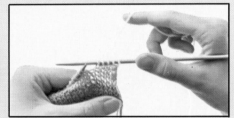

4 Take a ball of yarn in the third color and begin knitting with it. The ends of both the first and second colors are at the RH edge.

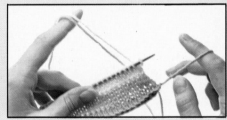

5 Complete four rows in the third color. Hold the needle with the stitches in your left hand ready to begin the next row with the first color. Untangle the first color and hold in your right hand: keep the other colors free at the back of the work.

6 Insert the RH needle into the first stitch to knit it. Wind the first color around the RH needle. Keep the loop of yarn at the RH edge fairly loose—pulling it tight distorts the row gauge. Work four rows as usual.

7 Continue in this way, changing color every four rows until the knitting is the depth you need. Don't let the ends of yarn become too tangled and keep the loops of yarn carried up the side at an even gauge.

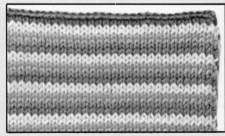

8 Cut off the two colors you have finished with, leaving 4in (10cm) ends (darn these in later). Bind off with the color used for the last stripe.

Horizontal stripes in garter and stockinette stitch

Simple stitches and colorful yarns combine to produce a variety of interesting effects in narrow horizontal stripes. Create your own design by using a pattern for a plain garter-stitch or stockinette-stitch garment, such as a sweater, and adding stripes to it. Unlike substituting one stitch for another, adding stripes to a pattern does not affect the gauge, so you need not worry about variations in size. Striping is also an ideal way to use up leftover yarn. Choose yarn of similar thicknesses for a neat, even fabric.

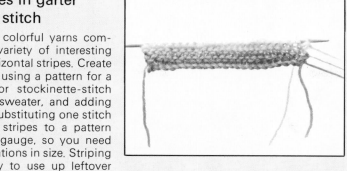

1 Choose three colors and knit an even number of rows with each (here there are two), carrying the yarns up the side of the work.

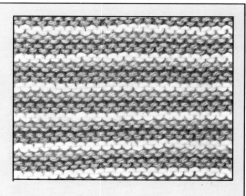

2 Note that the two rows in a single color form one horizontal ridge.

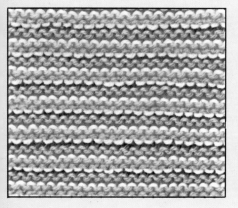

3 The reverse side of the garter-stitch fabric looks attractive and can be used as the right side of the work if you prefer. Each horizontal ridge here is a broken stripe made with two colors: these automatically form on the back as you change colors on the other side of the work.

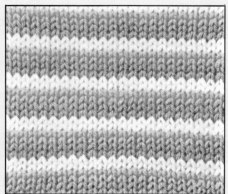

4 Here is the same 2-row stripe pattern worked in stockinette stitch. Change colors on a knit row to avoid lines of broken color on the right side of the work; in this way the yarns are always at the RH edge of the knitting so they can be carried up to the next stripe.

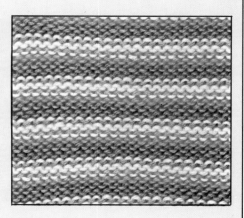

5 Broken stripes occur where you change colors on the reverse side of the stockinette-stitch fabric. It is similar to the garter-stitch version except that there is one row of plain-colored stitches separating the broken stripes.

Working narrow vertical stripes

To make a stockinette-stitch fabric with vertical stripes in two colors, you must use both balls of yarn within the same row of knitting. Each hand holds one color, and the color not in use is carried across the back of the work. Keep the strands loose so that the stitch gauge doesn't become distorted. This method of carrying yarn works only if the stripe is no more than five stitches wide; with more stitches the strands of carried yarn become too long and are likely to be caught and pulled. Carrying yarn on the wrong side produces a fabric that is double the normal thickness, making it ideal for heavier or outdoor garments.

1 To make a stockinette-stitch fabric with regular vertical stripes in 2 colors (A and B), cast on the required number of stitches with A. Wind B around the fingers of your left hand as shown.

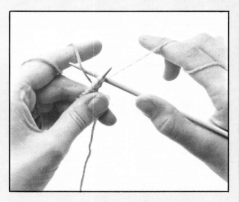

2 Hold needle with cast-on stitches in your left hand and wind A around the fingers of your right hand ready to begin knitting. The first stripe is in B: insert RH needle into first stitch, then from left to right under front of loop of yarn in B on left index finger.

continued

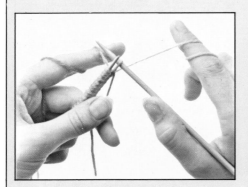

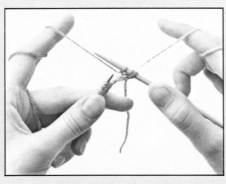

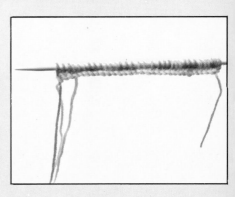

3 Twist RH needle forward so that yarn in B forms a loop around the needle. Use the RH needle to pull the loop in B through the stitch on the left-hand (LH) needle.

4 Allow the stitch in A to fall from the LH needle. Continue in this way, looping B through the required number of stitches (here it is 3) on the LH needle.

5 Knit the next 3 stitches with A in the usual way. Don't pull the yarn at the back of the work too tightly across the stitches in B. Work alternate stripes in B, then A, to end of row.

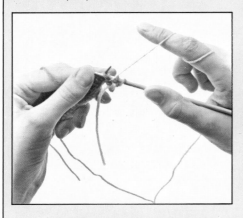

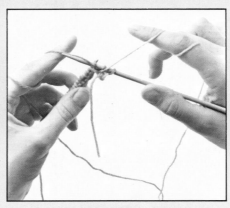

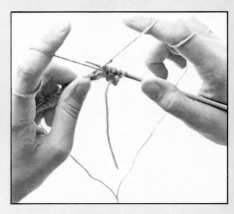

6 At the start of the second (purl) row, loop B around A to bring both yarns to RH edge. Holding yarns as before, wind B with your left hand from the front of the work over the top and around the RH needle point in a counterclockwise direction.

7 Pull a new loop in B through the stitch on the LH needle. Place the tip of your left thumb on the RH needle point as you pull it backward to help guide the new loop through the stitch and prevent its falling off the needle.

8 Allow the stitch to fall from the LH needle in the usual way. Work 3 stitches in B, then 3 in A, keeping B out of the way at the LH side of your work.

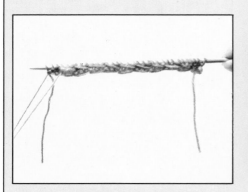

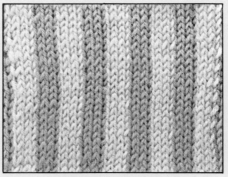

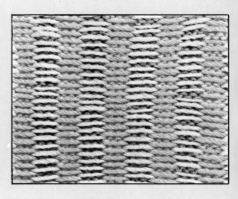

9 Purl to the end of the row, working the appropriate stitches in A and B. Keep checking that the yarn lies loosely across the wrong side of the knitting.

10 Always keeping A in your right hand and B in your left hand, work in stockinette stitch for the depth that you require. Bind off in the normal way using 1 color only.

11 The carried threads look very neat on the wrong side of the work: they have a regular under and over appearance without any twisting.

Joining shoulder seams

Most knitted garments are shaped to give a sloping line from the armhole edge up to the neck, along the shoulders. Patterns give specific instructions for shaping. Keep the continuity of the sloping line by joining the shoulder seams carefully.

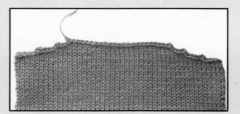

1 Begin shaping the shoulders 6 to 8 rows below the final group of bound-off stitches for the back neck. The bound-off stitches form an edge at each side, sloping from the armhole edge up to the stitches bound off in the center for the neck.

2 When the front is complete join the shoulder seams. Match bound-off edges right sides together, and pin in a straight line as shown. Sew with a back stitch seam following the line of pins.

Baby's own robe

Keep baby snug in this gaily colored robe, worked in horizontal and vertical stripes. Ribbon binding at the neck and front opening simplifies finishing, as does the ribbon-tie fastening.

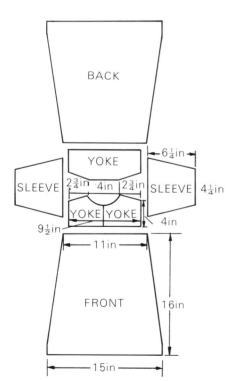

Sizes
To fit 18–20in (46–51cm) chest: other measurements are shown on the diagram.

Materials
Total of 8oz (200g) of a sport yarn
This garment took 2-3oz (60g) each in color A (pink) and B (ivory); 1-2oz (40g) each of 4 other colors, C (blue), D (green), E (red) and F (yellow)
1 pair each No. 2 (3mm) and 4 (3¾mm) needles
⅝yd (.5m) of ⅝in (1.5cm)-wide ribbon for binding
1⅛yd (1m) of ¼in (6mm)-wide ribbon for ties

Gauge
24 sts and 32 rows to 4in (10cm) over stockinette st worked on No. 4 (3¾mm) needles.

Horizontal stripe sequence
This consists of four rows each in colors F, C, B, E, D and A; repeat this sequence as directed in the pattern. Cut off yarn after finishing each color; the stripes are too wide to carry yarn up the side.

Skirt back
☐ Using No. 2 (3mm) needles and A, cast on 92 sts. Work 4 rows garter st.
☐ Change to No. 4 (3¾mm) needles. Beginning with a K row, continue in stockinette st and horizontal stripe sequence.
☐ Dec one st at each end of 25th and then every 8th row until 68 sts remain.
☐ Work 116 rows in stripes, finishing after last row of D in the 5th repeat.
☐ Change to No. 2 (3mm) needles.

Using A, work 4 rows garter st. Bind off.

Skirt front
☐ Work as given for skirt back.

Sleeves
☐ Using No. 2 (3mm) needles and A, cast on 28 sts. Work 4 rows garter st.
☐ Change to No. 4 (3¾mm) needles. Beginning with a K row, continue in stockinette st and stripe sequence.
☐ Inc one st at each end of 5th and then every 4th row until there are 48 sts.
☐ Work a total of 44 rows in stripes, finishing after last row of D in the 2nd repeat.
☐ Change to No. 2 (3mm) needles. Using A, work 4 rows garter st. Bind off.

Yoke back
☐ Using No. 4 (3¾mm) needles and B, cast on 57 sts.
☐ Begin vertical stripe pattern. Using B, K3 sts, using A, K3 sts; alternately K3 sts using B and A to end of row.
☐ Continue in stockinette st and vertical stripes as above until work measures 4in (10cm), ending with a P row.
☐ Bind off 4 sts at beginning of each of next 8 rows to shape shoulders.
☐ Bind off remaining 35 sts.

Yoke left front
☐ Using No. 4 (3¾mm) needles and B, cast on 29 sts.

Diagram labels:
BACK
YOKE
SLEEVE — 6¼in
2¾in — 4in — 2¾in — SLEEVE — 4¼in
YOKE YOKE — 4in
9½in
11in
FRONT — 16in
15in

□ Begin vertical stripe pattern. Using B, K3 sts, using A, K3 sts; alternately K3 sts using B and A to last 5 sts, using B, K3 sts, using A, K2 sts.

□ Continue in vertical stripes until there are 11 rows less than back before the shoulder shaping, ending at front edge.

□ Shape neck by binding off at beginning of next and every other row (i.e. same edge at start of P rows) 6 sts once, 2 sts twice, one st 3 times. The last row is a P row and 16 sts remain.

□ Bind off at the beginning of next and every other row (i.e. same edge at start of K rows) 4 sts 4 times to shape shoulders.

Yoke right front

□ Using No. 4 (3¾mm) needles and B, cast on 29 sts.

□ Begin vertical stripe pattern. Using A, K2 sts, using B, K3 sts, using A, K3 sts; alternately K3 sts using B and A to end of row, finishing with 3 sts in B.

□ Continue in vertical stripes until there are 10 rows less than back before the shoulder shaping, ending at front edge.

□ Continue as given for left front yoke, reversing position of neck shaping by binding off at beginning of K rows. Reverse shoulder shaping by binding off at beginning of P rows.

To finish

□ Press or block according to yarn used.

□ Using a back stitch seam throughout, join shoulder seams.

□ Mark center of sleeve top with a pin and match to shoulder seam. Sew sleeve tops in position along sides of yoke.

□ Sew yoke to top of skirt, easing skirt slightly to fit yoke.

□ Join side and sleeve seams. Press finished seams.

□ Bind neck and front opening with ribbon. Sew on ribbon ties at top of front opening.

Knitting / COURSE 12

Knitting a background for smocking

Smocking is a technique normally used in dressmaking to control fullness in a fabric: similar techniques applied to knitting are particularly successful since knitted fabrics are naturally elastic. Garments knitted in fine yarns lend themselves to smocking; those made of thick yarns are too bulky. A ribbed fabric is a perfect background for smocking, as the vertical knit ribs serve as a guide for the stitching. The most popular back-ground is single knit ribs with three stitches between them. To make a fabric of the required width after smocking you must first knit one measuring one and a half times the finished width. Specific details, including the number of stitches, normally appear in a pattern. The following steps can be used in working your own design for a smocked panel for a bodice, yoke or cuffs on a dress or blouse.

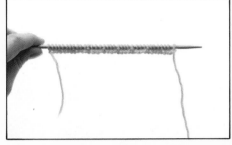

1 Make a gauge sample to calculate the number of stitches required. Cast on a multiple of 8 stitches (e.g. 16, 24, 32) plus 3 extra stitches. Try 35 stitches for knitting worsted. To work the row (this is the right side of the fabric), P3 sts. K3 alternately until 3 sts remain, P3.

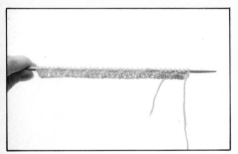

2 To work the 2nd row K3 sts, then P1 st alternately until 3 sts remain. K3. The wrong side of the work is facing you.

3 Repeat the two pattern rows until the fabric is about 2½in (6cm) deep, ending with a 2nd row.

4 Bind off, keeping the rib sequence correct.

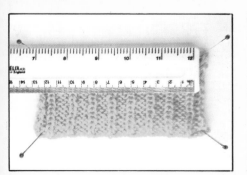

5 Pin the sample down and measure 4in (10cm) across the center. Count the number of stitches to 4in (10cm); on our sample it is 25.

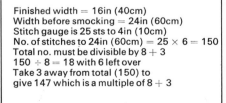

Finished width = 16in (40cm)
Width before smocking = 24in (60cm)
Stitch gauge is 25 sts to 4in (10cm)
No. of stitches to 24in (60cm) = 25 × 6 = 150
Total no. must be divisible by 8 + 3
150 ÷ 8 = 18 with 6 left over
Take 3 away from total (150) to
give 147 which is a multiple of 8 + 3

6 Calculate the number of stitches to cast on. For example, if you want the completed work to measure 16in (40cm) across, use the figures given here to determine the number of cast-on stitches.

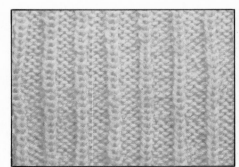

7 Cast on the necessary number of stitches and make the background fabric the depth you require. The vertical ribs are an ideal guide for the smocking.

Smocking a knitted fabric

After the background fabric is finished, work horizontal lines of stitching across it using a contrasting yarn of the same quality. The stitching draws pairs of ribs together across the fabric: their position alternates on every other row to form the characteristic honeycomb effect.

1 To work the 1st row, locate the stitch on the 2nd rib from right-hand (RH) edge in the 4th row. Thread a blunt-ended yarn needle with the smocking thread; secure with 2 or 3 small stitches, one on top of another, on the wrong side.

2 Bring needle from back to front just before the 2nd knit rib: reinsert from front to back after 3rd knit rib. The strand of yarn covers 5 stitches—2 knit ribs and 3 purl stitches between them.

3 Wind yarn once or twice around the stitches again, finishing with the needle at the back. Pull yarn gently, drawing the ribs together.

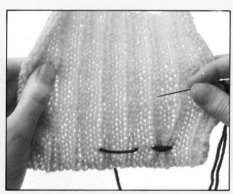

4 Carrying yarn across back of work, bring needle from back to front immediately before the next knit rib to the left. Skip this rib, 3 purl stitches and following rib; reinsert needle from front to back.

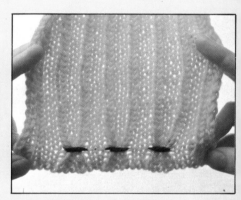

5 Continue in this way, winding yarn around pairs of ribs and drawing them together until 1st row is complete. Fasten off.

6 To work 2nd row, first skip 4 rows; rejoin yarn behind 1st rib at RH edge. Bring needle from back to front just before the 1st rib; reinsert from front to back after 2nd rib (i.e. 1st rib of 1st pair drawn together on previous row).

7 Wind yarn around the stitches again, finishing with the needle at the back. Pull yarn gently drawing the ribs together. Continue in the same way as on the previous row, always taking left-hand (LH) rib of pair below together with RH rib of the next pair.

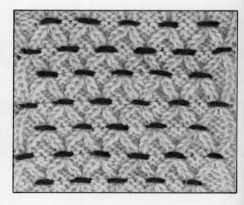

8 Always skipping 4 rows between lines of smocking, work 1st and 2nd rows alternately for the depth you require. The lines of stitching draw the ribs together into a textured honeycomb pattern.

Knitting in smocking

Rather than adding smocking after the background is finished, you can add it simultaneously while working the background. Use a cable needle to hold the stitches to be drawn together separate from the remainder of the work while you wind the smocking thread around them. Keep the strands of yarn threaded loosely across the wrong side of the background; draw them up when you have finished all the rows of smocking.

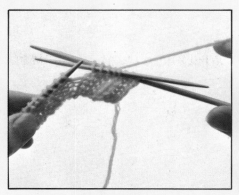

1 Cast on a multiple of 8 stitches (e.g. 16, 24, 32) plus 3 extra stitches. Work 4 rows in rib (see steps 1 and 2 of "Knitting a background for smocking").
To work the 1st row of smocking, knit the first 8 stitches in pattern. Take a cable needle and insert it from left to right through the front of the last 5 sts.

2 Withdraw the right-hand (RH) needle from the stitches on the cable needle. Position the cable needle at the front of the work with other needles behind it.

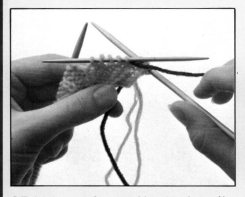

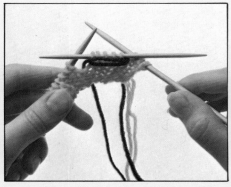

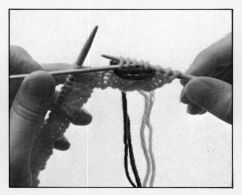

3 Take the yarn for smocking, leaving a 4in (10cm) end, from the back of the work to the front between the RH needle and cable needle.

4 Use your right hand to wind the yarn for smocking twice around the front of the 5 stitches on the cable needle in a clockwise direction. Leave the yarn at the back of the work.

5 Insert the RH needle from right to left through the stitches on the cable needle. Withdraw the cable needle returning the 5 stitches to the RH needle.

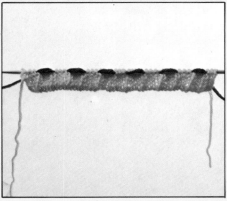

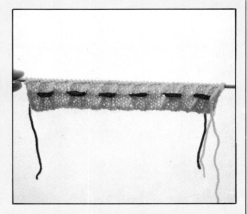

6 Leaving the smocking yarn at the back of the work, pattern another 8 stitches of background. Draw the ribs together at a later stage.

7 Repeat these steps threading the smocking yarn across the back of the work until you reach the end of the row. Cut off the smocking yarn leaving a 4in (10cm) end.

8 Pattern 3 rows: you can vary the number of rows between smocking as long as it is uneven (3, 5, 7). The right side of the work faces you as you start the 2nd smocking row.

continued

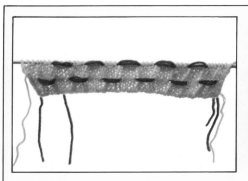

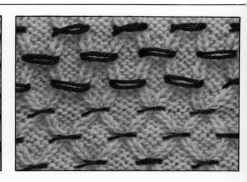

9 To work 2nd smocking row, pattern 12 stitches before slipping the last 5 stitches worked onto a cable needle and winding around them the smocking yarn as before. Note that 1 knit rib at each end is left unworked and the smocked stitches alternate with those in the 1st row.

10 Continue in pattern with smocking rows (alternate 1st and 2nd smocking rows) at regular intervals until the fabric is the depth you require. Work 3 rows of rib after last smocking row. Bind off in ribbed pattern.

11 Draw up each row of smocking: secure the smocking yarn on the back of the work at one edge. Gently pull the ribs together individually before securing at the opposite edge.

More abbreviations to learn

K=knit
P=purl
st(s)=stitch(es)
K1, P1 rib=knit 1, purl 1 (single rib)

At left are the abbreviations that you already know; most refer to special knitting techniques. To keep directions short and concise, a number of frequently used ordinary words are abbreviated to form part of the special knitting shorthand. Here is a list of some of these words in alphabetical order: they will now appear in the patterns in the knitting courses so that you can become familiar with them.

beg=begin(ning)
dec=decrease(e)(ing)
inc=increas(e)(ing)
patt=pattern
rem=remain(ing)
rep=repeat
tog=together

Pretty-up for a party

A charming silky, smocked dress like this will be a big hit at party time. The smocking gives it a delicate, traditional look, but the dress will stand up to plenty of wear and tear.

Sizes
To fit 20[22:24]in (51[56:61]cm) chest. The figures in brackets [] refer to the 2nd and 3rd sizes respectively.

Materials
Total of 7[8:8]oz (180[200:220g) of a silky rayon yarn
Extra yarn in 2 colors for embroidery, or left-over embroidery thread
1 pair each Nos, 1 and 2 (2½ and 3mm) knitting needles
1¾yd (1.5m) of ribbon for ties
Tapestry needle

Gauge
30 sts and 40 rows to 4in (10cm) over stockinette st on No. 2 (3mm) needles.

Front
☐ Using No. 1 (2½mm) needles cast on 193 [201:209] sts. Work 4 rows garter st.
☐ Change to No. 2 (3mm) needles. Beg with a K row, continue in stockinette st until work measures 1½in (4cm) from beg, ending with a P row.
☐ Continue in ribbed pattern for background. An asterisk *, in a pattern row is another form of knitting shorthand: it means repeat the sequence of stitches following it as directed.
☐ To work the next row P2 sts, *K1 st, P3 sts, rep from * (i.e. K1 st and P3 sts alternately) to last 3 sts, K1 st, P2 sts.
☐ To work the following row K2 sts, *P1 st, K3 sts, rep from * to last 3 sts, P1 st, K2 sts.
☐ Rep the last 2 rows 8 times more, then the first row again (19 rows in all).
☐ Change to No. 1 (2½mm) needles. To work the next row K3 sts. *K3 sts tog, K5 sts, rep from * to last 6 sts, K3 sts tog, K3 sts. 145[151:157] sts rem.
☐ Work 4 rows garter st. Change to No. 2 (3mm) needles. To work the next row K1 [2:3] sts, *K2 sts tog, K3[3:4]

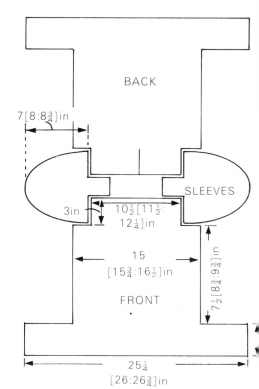

BACK

7[8:8¾]in

SLEEVES

3in

10½[11½:12¼]in

15 [15¾:16½]in

FRONT

7½[8¼:9¾]in

25¼ [26:26¾]in

Kim Sayer

opening, reversing rib and shaping.

Sleeves

☐ Using No. 1 (2½mm) needles cast on 18[24:30] sts for neck edge of shoulder section. Work 4 rows garter st.

☐ Change to No. 2 (3mm) needles. Beg with a K row, continue in stockinette st until work measures 3[3½:4]in (8[9:10] cm) from beg, ending with a P row.

☐ Shape sleeve by casting on 24 sts at beg of next 2 rows. K next row to last 2 sts, leave these sts unworked; turn and P following row to last 2 sts, leave these sts unworked; turn and K next row to last 4 sts, leave these sts unworked. Continue to work 2 sts less on every row until 6[8:10] sts rem in center, then K to end.

☐ Change to No 1 (2½mm) needles. Work 4 rows garter st. Bind off.

sts, K2 tog, K2[3:3] sts, rep from * to end, but on 2nd size only finish with K2 sts. 113[121:129] sts rem.

☐ Beg with a K row, continue in stockinette st until work measures 11½[12¾:13¾]in (29[32:35]cm) from beg, ending with a P row**

☐ Work 31 rows in ribbed pattern as before, ending with right side facing.

☐ Change to No. 1 (2½mm) needles. To work the next row K3 sts, *K3 sts tog, K5, rep from * to last 6 sts, K3 sts tog, K3 sts 85[91:97] sts rem.

☐ Work 3 rows garter st. Bind off.

Back

☐ Work as given for front until you reach the point in the directions marked with a double asterisk, **. Now follow the directions given here.

☐ To divide for the back opening, work 54[58:62] sts in rib, then K2 sts, slip rem sts on left-hand (LH) needle on a stitch holder, turn and continue on first set of 56[60:64] sts.

☐ To work the following row K2 sts, rib to end of row. Work 29 more rows, ending with right side of work facing. Change to No. 1 (2½mm) needles.

☐ To work the next row K2[6:2] sts, *K3 sts tog, K5 sts, rep from * to last 6 sts, K3 sts tog, K3 sts. 40[44:46] sts.

☐ Work 3 rows garter st. Bind off.

☐ Return to sts on stitch holder and slip them back onto LH needle. With right side of work facing, rejoin yarn to first st, K2 sts tog, K1 st, rib to end.

☐ Complete to match other side of

To finish

☐ Block pieces of knitting to correct size. Lightly dampen with fine spray and leave to dry.

☐ Starting from top of ribbed background on yoke, work smocking on every 6th row alternating lines of stitching in two different colors.

☐ Beg at armhole edges and using a back stitch seam throughout, sew straight edges of sleeves to bound-off edges of back and front.

☐ Sew cast-on sts at each side of sleeves to sides of smocking on back and front. Join side seams.

☐ Work smocking on skirt.

☐ Press all seams with a cool iron and a damp cloth.

☐ Sew on ribbons to form ties at top of center back opening.

Knitting / COURSE 13

Casting on with one needle

Try this quick and simple method of casting on; you may prefer it to the two-needle method. It produces a firm but elastic edge suitable for most general knitting purposes.

Use a single needle from the pair required for the knitting: hold it in your right hand to make and hold the cast-on stitches.

Your left thumb acts as a flexible "needle" for winding the yarn around and forming stitches.

1 Make a slipknot with a loop in the yarn some distance from the end. The short end of yarn is for making the cast-on stitches—40in (1m) knitting worsted yarn makes approximately 60 stitches. Place the loop on the needle.

2 Hold the needle in the normal way in your right hand. Insert your left thumb under the shorter end of yarn from the back so that the yarn travels in a counterclockwise direction from the loop around the thumb.

3 Hold the yarn around your thumb down across your left palm with the fingers of that hand, keeping the index finger free for working. Wind the yarn from the main ball around the fingers of your right hand in the usual way.

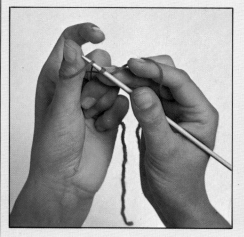

4 Use your left thumb as a form of needle: insert the needle into the loop on the part of the thumb facing you.

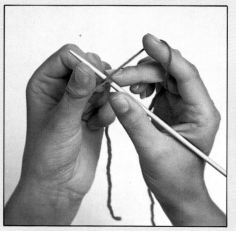

5 Wind the yarn from the main ball under and over the needle point in a clockwise direction.

6 Draw a loop of yarn through the loop on your thumb to form a new stitch on the needle.

Fred Mancini

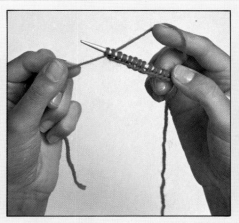

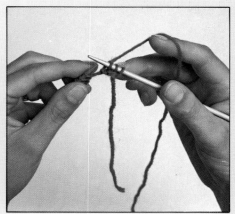

7 Withdraw your thumb from the loop of yarn around it. Pull the short end of yarn gently to tighten the stitch on the needle.

8 Continue to wind the yarn from the short end around your left thumb. Work as described in steps 4 to 7 until you have cast on the required number of stitches.

9 Transfer the needle with the cast-on stitches to your left hand. Take the second needle in your right hand and begin knitting in the usual way. There are two ends of yarn at the beginning of your first row: remember to knit with the yarn from the main ball.

Decreasing by working two stitches together through the back of the loops

Often when shaping a simple raglan arm-hole you must knit two stitches together through the back of the loops — abbreviated as "K2 tog tbl." This type of decrease is often found at the end of right-side rows — sometimes within a one- or two-stitch border: it produces a neat edge with a distinctive slope to the right. The same technique can also be applied to purl stitches.

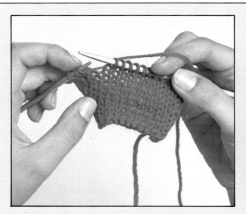

1 On the right side of a stockinette stitch fabric, knit to the position of the decrease—in this case when 3 stitches remain on the left-hand needle.

2 Insert right-hand needle from right to left through back of next 2 stitches.

3 Knit the 2 stitches together in the usual way—called K2 tog tbl—; knit the last stitch.

4 A line of this type of decrease on every knit row has a neat appearance with a distinctive slant to the stitches.

5 To purl 2 stitches together through the back of the loops—P2 tog tbl—insert the right-hand needle from left to right through the back of the 2 stitches. Purl the stitches together in the usual way.

Fred Mancini

37

Cross-stitch

Cross-stitch is an effective way to embroider a stockinette-stitch fabric. Apply the stitching after the fabric is complete, but plan the design beforehand. Each cross covers a square section of background; each square has slightly more stitches than rows. By covering two stitches and three rows of knitting, or three stitches and four rows, you make small and large crosses respectively.

The position of the needle as you work is important; always insert it to the side of the stitches over which you are working. If you insert the needle through the center of a stitch, the natural elasticity of the knitting pulls the embroidery out of shape.

1 Mark the area to be embroidered with pins inserted after every four rows and between every three stitches. The evening cardigan in this course has an additional two free rows between lines of crosses.

2 Using a blunt-ended yarn needle threaded with sewing thread, baste lines of stitches on the background to form a grid of squares. Each square will eventually have a cross covering it.

3 Thread a blunt-ended needle with your chosen yarn. Yarn used for embroidery on knitting is usually similar in thickness to the background yarn. Secure yarn to back of work at lower right corner of design (this is on the left when the wrong side of the work is facing you).

4 Bring needle from back to front at side of first marked stitch (i.e. *between* this stitch and next stitch to the right) at lower corner of first box.

5 Working from right to left, reinsert needle from front to back after third stitch four rows above—at corner of box diagonally opposite where yarn is joined.

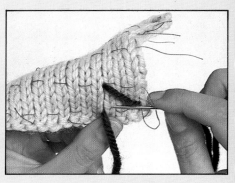

6 Bring needle to front again at lower right corner of next box to the left, making sure that you always insert the needle between stitches.

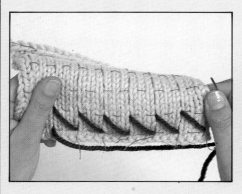

7 Continue in this way, working one diagonal line of each cross, until you reach the end of the first line of pattern. Finish with the yarn at the lower left corner of the last box.

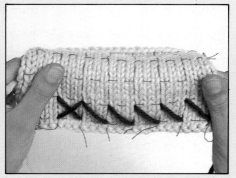

8 Working from left to right, reinsert the needle from front to back at corner of box diagonally opposite. One cross-stitch is complete.

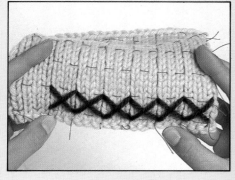

9 Bring the needle to the front again at lower left corner of next box to the right. Repeat steps 8 and 9 to complete first line of crosses.

Fred Mancini

Chain stitch

Chain stitch looks best worked in a contrasting color against a stockinette-stitch background. It is particularly effective as horizontal and vertical lines dividing the background into large checks. To keep the checks square you must work individual chains over slightly more rows than stitches. The chains on the checked jacket included in this chapter are worked over two stitches and three rows. This can be varied according to the thickness of the knitted yarn; some finer yarns may require chains to be worked over every stitch horizontally and every two rows vertically.

1 Using a blunt-ended yarn needle threaded with sewing thread, baste lines of stitches on the background to form a guide for the embroidery. Work vertical lines through center of knitted stitches and horizontal lines across the stitches of one row of knitting.

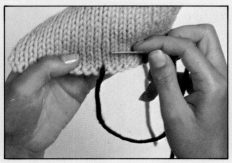

2 Thread a blunt-ended needle with yarn for the embroidery; this is usually similar in thickness to the background. Secure yarn to the back of work at lower edge of marked vertical line. Bring needle from back to front through center of first stitch and pull yarn through.

3 Form the yarn into a wide circle above the line of stitching. Hold the yarn with your left thumb; reinsert the needle through the center of the corresponding stitch three rows above.

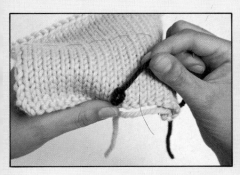

4 Pull the yarn through, drawing the large circle in to make one chain stitch. Keep the embroidery yarn loose so that it does not pucker the knitted background.

5 Repeat the process of making chains over every three rows until the line of embroidery is the length you need. Insert the needle from front to back immediately above last stitch worked and fasten off on the back of the work.

6 To embroider horizontal lines, turn work so that side edge of background becomes the lower edge. Secure yarn to back of work at lower edge of marked line. Bring needle from back to front between first and second stitches.

7 Form the yarn into a wide circle above the line of stitching and hold yarn down with your left thumb. Reinsert the needle between the first and second stitches and out again after the third stitch.

8 Pull the yarn through, drawing the large circle in to make one chain stitch. Make chains over every two stitches until the line of embroidery is the length you need. Fasten off on the wrong side.

9 On a large piece of fabric, work all the lines in the same direction first; in this way the lines of chain always cross in the same order.

Fred Mancini

Evening sparkle

Add a little sparkle to your evenings with this attractive cover-up. Cross-stitches worked over the knitted fabric form intriguing pyramids around the sleeves and the lower front edge. The borders are in garter stitch.

Sizes
To fit 32½[34:36:38]in (83[87:92:97] cm) bust; other measurements are shown on the diagram. The figures in brackets [] refer to the 2nd, 3rd and 4th sizes respectively.

Materials
Total of 10[11:11:12]oz (275[300: 300:325]g) of glitter yarn
Extra yarn in another color for embroidery
1 pair each Nos. 1 and 3 (2½ and 3¼mm) knitting needles

Gauge
28 sts and 36 rows to 4in (10cm) over stockinette st on No. 3 (3¼mm) needles.

Back
Using No. 1 (2½mm) needles cast on 114[122:130:138] sts. Work 10 rows garter st.
☐ Change to No. 3 (3¼mm) needles. Beg with a K row, continue in stockinette st until work measures 16in (41cm) from beg, ending with a P row.
☐ Beg armhole shaping by binding off 7 sts at beg of next 2 rows.
☐ To work the next row, K1 st, K2 sts tog, K to last 3 sts, K2 sts tog tbl, K1 st. To work the following row, P to end.
☐ Rep the last 2 rows until 34[36:38:40] sts rem, ending with a P row. Bind off.

Left front
Using No. 1 (2½mm) needles cast on 57[61:65:69] sts. Work 10 rows garter st.
☐ Change to No. 3 (3¼mm) needles. Beg with a K row, continue in stockinette st until work measures same as back to armholes, ending with a P row.
☐ Begin shaping armhole by binding off 7 sts at beg of next row. P following row.
☐ Shape front edge at same time as armhole edge: to work the next row K1 st, K2 sts tog, K to last 3 sts (front edge), K2 sts tog tbl, K1 st.
☐ Continue to dec at front edge on every 4th row 14[15:16:17] times more, *at the same time* dec at armhole edge on every other row until 2sts rem, ending with a P row. Bind off.

Right front
Work to match left front, reversing shaping at armhole and front edges by ending with K row before beg armhole shaping; omit P row following row where you bound off 7 sts for underarm and start front edge shaping on next row.

Sleeves
Using No. 1 (2½mm) needles cast on 78 [84:88:94] sts. Work 10 rows garter st.
☐ Change to No. 3 (3¼mm) needles. Beg with a K row, continue in stockinette st, inc one st at each end of 5th and every foll 6th row to 90[96:100:106] sts.
☐ Continue without shaping until sleeve measures 4¾in (12cm) down center of sleeve from beg, ending with a P row.
☐ Beg shaping raglan sleeve top by binding off 7 sts at beg of next 2 rows.
☐ Rep the 2 rows of back armhole shaping until 10[10:8:8] sts rem, ending with a P row. Bind off.

Front border
Using No. 1 (2½mm) needles cast on 8 sts.
☐ Work in garter st until border reaches up front edge, around back neck and down other front. Bind off.

Ties (make 2)
Using No. 1 (2½mm) needles cast on 6 sts. Work in garter st for 10in (25cm). Bind off.

To finish
☐ Join all raglan seams using a back-stitch seam. Join side and sleeve seams.
☐ Using a flat seam, sew on front border. Sew ties in position.
☐ Work cross-stitch embroidery. First row, over 3 sts and 4 rows, goes around lower edge, 5 rows above garter st border.
☐ On each front work a pyramid of 10, 8, 6, 4 and 2 crosses with 2 rows of knitting between each line.
☐ Work a similar pattern on both the sleeves.

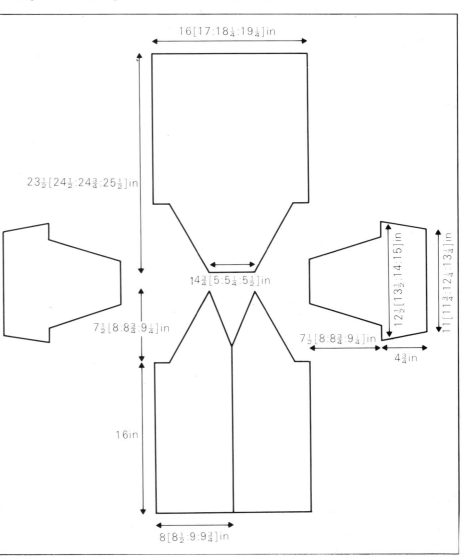

16[17:18¼:19¼]in

23½[24½:24¾:25½]in

14¾[5:5¼:5½]in

7½[8:8¾:9¼]in

16in

8[8½:9:9¾]in

12½[13:14:15]in

11[11½:12:13¼]in

7½[8:8¾:9¼]in

4¾in

Brian Mayor

Checks, chains and crosses

A simple jacket in stockinette stitch takes on an ethnic look with the addition of cross-stitch and chain stitch embroidery.

Sizes
To fit 32½[34:36:38]in (83[87:92:97] cm)·bust: other measurements are on the diagram below.
The figures in brackets [ ] refer to the 2nd, 3rd and 4th sizes respectively.

Materials
Total of 18[20:22:23]oz (500[550: 600:650]g) of a knitting worsted
Extra yarn in two contrasting colors for embroidery
1 pair each Nos. 5 and 7 (4 and 5mm) knitting needles

Gauge
16 sts and 22 rows to 4in (10cm) over stockinette st on No. 7 (5mm) needles. If your gauge is wrong, use a different needle size.

Back
Using No. 5 (4mm) needles cast on 70 [74:78:82] sts. Work 8 rows garter st.
☐ Change to No. 7 (5mm) needles. Beg with a K row, continue in stockinette st until work measures 17¾in (45cm) from beg, ending with a P row.
☐ Beg armhole shaping by binding off 3 sts at beg of next 2 rows.
☐ To work the next row, K1 st, K2 sts tog, K to last 3 sts, K2 sts tog tbl, K1 st. To work the following row, P to end.
☐ Rep the last 2 rows until 20[20:22:22] sts rem, ending with a P row. Bind off.

Left front
Using No. 5 (4mm) needles cast on 35[37:39:41] sts. Work 8 rows garter st.
☐ Change to No. 7 (5mm) needles. Beg with a K row, continue in stockinette st until work measures same as back to

armholes ending with a P row.
☐ Beg armhole shaping by binding off 13 sts at beg of next row. P the next row.
☐ Shape front edge at same time as armhole edge: to work the next row K1 st, K2 sts tog, K to last 3 sts (front edge), K2 sts tog tbl, K1 st.
☐ Continue to dec at front edge on every 4th row 7[7:8:8] times more, *at the same time* dec at armhole edge on every other row until 2 sts rem, ending with a P row. Bind off.

Right front
Work to match left front, reversing shaping at armhole and front edges by ending with a K row before beg armhole shaping; omit the P row following row where you bound off 3 sts for underarm and start front edge shaping on next row.

Sleeves
Using No. 5 (4mm) needles cast on 36[38:40:42] sts. Work 8 rows garter st.
☐ Change to No. 7 (5mm) needles. Beg with a K row, work in stockinette st, inc one at each end of 7th and every foll 6th row until there are 58[62:64:68] sts.
☐ Continue without shaping until sleeve measures 17[17¼:17¾:18]in (43[44:45: 46]cm) in a straight line down centre of sleeve from beg, ending with a P row.
☐ Beg shaping raglan sleeve top by binding off 3 sts at beg of next 2 rows.
☐ Rep the 2 rows of back armhole shaping until 8 sts rem, ending with a P row. Bind off.

Front border
Using No. 5 (4mm) needles cast on 6 sts.
☐ Work in garter st until band reaches up front edge, around back neck and down other front. Bind off.

Ties (make 2)
Using No. 5 (4mm) needles cast on 4 sts. Work in garter st for 10in (25cm). Bind off.

To finish
Press (except garter st borders and ties) with a dry cloth and a cool iron.
☐ Work chain stitch embroidery, dividing pieces of knitting into large checks: see diagram for approximate position of lines. As far as possible, divide the area equally so that there are about the same number of sts and rows in each check.
☐ Use first contrast color to work a cross-stitch over center 3 sts and 4 rows of each check. With 2nd contrast color work 4 more crosses 2 sts and 4 rows distant from the first cross.
☐ Join all raglan seams using a backstitch. Join side and sleeve seams.
☐ Using a flat seam, sew on front border. Sew ties in position. Press.

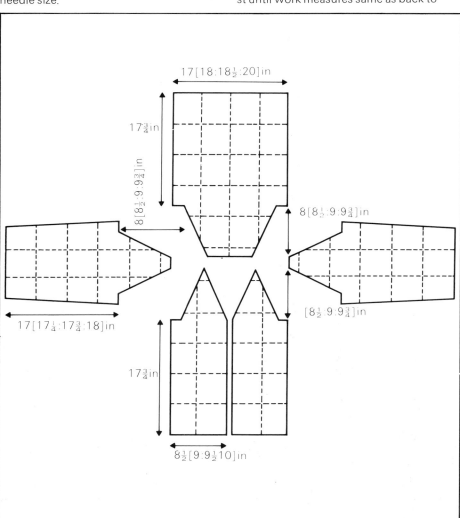

17[18:18½:20]in

17¾in

8[8½:9:9¾]in

8[8½:9:9¾]in

17[17¼:17¾:18]in

17¾in

8½[9:9½:10]in

[8½:9:9¾]in

Shoestring

Playtime

Let the children play with their toys on this bright play mat; when they've finished just pull up the cords to put the toys away.

Materials

1yd (.9m) of 36in (90cm)-wide sailcloth
⅝ to 1yd (.5 to 1m) of a bold animal or toy-printed cotton fabric from which large motifs can be cut
Matching thread
Eighteen ¾in (2cm)-diameter white plastic curtain rings
4⅜yd (4m) of white cord
Embroidery hoop
Thumbtack, string and chalk

1 Fold the 36in (90cm) square in half one way and then in half again the opposite way. Pin the edges together to hold. Place the folded square on the floor.
2 Tie a piece of string around a thumbtack. Fix this thumbtack to the corner point which is the centre of the fabric when it is unfolded. Tie the other end of the string around a piece of chalk, so that the string reaches the length of one of the sides. Holding the thumbtack in place, carefully draw the chalk in an arc from one corner to the other, keeping the string taut.
3 Remove the thumbtack. Pin the four layers of fabric together just inside the chalk line. Cut through all four layers of fabric around marked chalk line to make a large circle.
4 Turn under a double ⅜in (1cm) hem. Pin, baste and stitch in place.
5 Cut out motifs from the printed fabric, leaving at least a ¾in (2cm) border around each one.
6 Arrange the motifs around the edge of the fabric circle, positioning them about 1½in (4cm) in from the outer edge.
7 Pin and baste them to the circle, making sure they are smoothed flat.
8 Set your machine to satin stitch, with a width of about 3/16 in (4mm). Place the first motif to be worked in the embroidery hoop, with part of the edge to be sewn inside the hoop. The fabric layers in the hoop need not be very taut but must be of equal tension. Work around the outline of the motif, re-positioning the hoop as necessary.
9 Continue, sewing around each motif in turn.
10 Draw all loose ends of thread to the wrong side and tie off.
11 With sharp-pointed scissors, cut away the extra fabric very carefully from around each motif.
12 Sew the curtain rings around the edge of the circle, spacing them evenly.
13 Thread the cord through the rings and knot the ends together.

Rupert Watts

*Checking measurements
 for T-shaped designs
*Adapting T-shaped pieces
*Planning your own design
*Single crochet edging
*Patterns for 3 children's
 sweaters

Checking measurements for T-shaped designs

In this chapter we introduce the popular T-shaped design – easy to make and almost as easy to vary to suit your own taste and requirements. The name, of course, derives from the way the garment, with arms outstretched, resembles a large letter T.

Patterns for three children's T-shaped sweaters are given on page 51; these step-by-step directions show you how to check the child's measurements, and if necessary, how to alter the pattern accordingly.

The diagram shows the pieces required for the children's sweaters – basically there are two shapes – the back and front are alike and so are the sleeves. The measurement chart gives a number of measurements on the sweaters that vary according to the chest size. First measure the child's chest size without garments on. Find this size on the chart and check that the other measurements for this size are suitable; if not, they can be altered to suit a particular child's requirements by lengthening or shortening the body and sleeves.

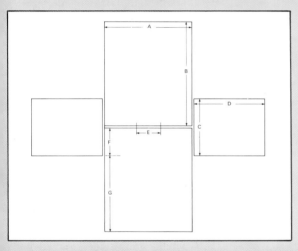

Chest Size	Code on diagram	20in	22in	24in	26in	28in	30in
Width across front/back	A	11in	11¾in	13in	14in	15in	15¾in
Total length of sweater	B	11½in	13in	14½in	16in	17¾in	19¼in
Width around sleeve	C	8¼in	9in	10¼in	11in	12¼in	13in
Sleeve length	D	7in	8½in	10in	11½in	12¾in	14¼in
Approx width of neck opening	E	6in	6¼in	6¾in	7in	7½in	8in
Armhole depth	F	4⅛in	4½in	5⅛in	5½in	6⅛in	6½in
Underarm length front/back	G	7¼in	8½in	9½in	10⅝in	11⅝in	12¾in

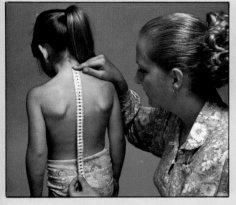

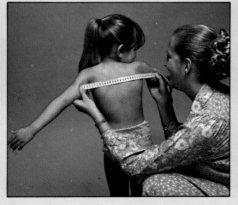

Fred Mancini

1 Referring to the pattern, note the finished length of the sweater for the chest size you are making. Check this against the child, placing the beginning of the tape against the center-back neck and measuring downward.

2 To check the sleeve measurement the child should stand with arms outstretched. Hold the tape with back measurement across shoulders and note where side edge of sweater will fall on arms; this is called a dropped shoulder line.

3 Measure the sleeve length from the dropped shoulder line downward along the arm. For a short sleeve, subtract the necessary amount: make the sleeve longer for a turn-back cuff by adding extra length. (You can work to the length given and then turn back a cuff, as on the garter-stitch sweater, but this shortens the length of the sleeve.)

Adapting the basic T-shaped pieces

You can easily alter a T-shaped pattern in several ways. For example, you can vary the direction of the knitting: instead of knitting the body and sleeve pieces from lower edge to top, as you normally would, you can knit them from one side edge to the other. You can knit the body vertically and the sleeves horizontally, or vice versa. Choose garter stitch, with its definite ridges, if you want to create strong directional emphasis.

It is also fairly easy to alter the lengths of basic pieces, making them longer or shorter where necessary to suit individual requirements.

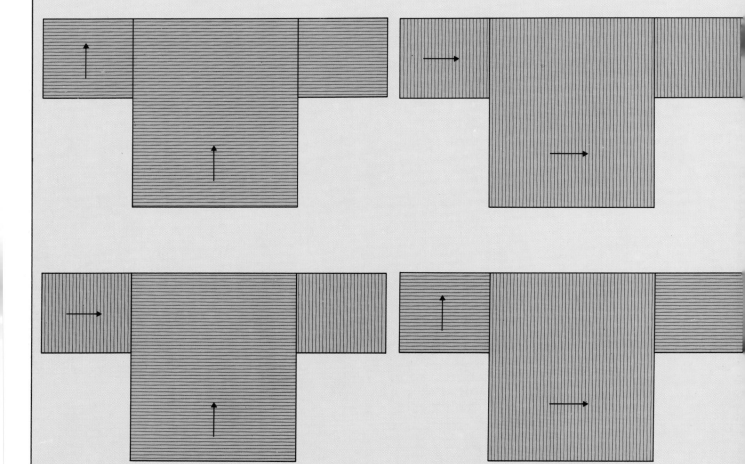

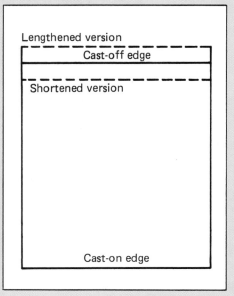

Lengthened version

Cast-off edge

Shortened version

Cast-on edge

1 If you are working the back and front of a sweater from the lower edge to top and want to lengthen or shorten it, simply work to the measurement you require.

2 To lengthen or shorten a sleeve knitted from wrist to top edge, work to the length you require then bind off. Extra length for a turn-back cuff is added in the same way.

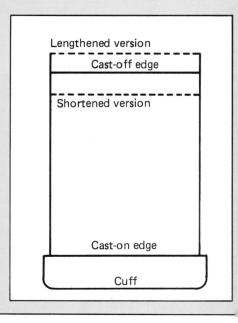

Lengthened version

Cast-off edge

Shortened version

Cast-on edge

Cuff

Total length of sweater = 17¾in (45cm)

Number of cast-on stitches for side edge = 54

You want to add 2in (5cm) in length

Look at the stitch gauge; in this pattern it is 12 stitches to 4in (10cm)

Here an extra 6 stitches give the extra 2in (5cm) required.
Cast on (54 + 6) 60 stitches in all.

3 Altering the length of a sweater is more difficult if you are working from side edge to side edge: here the number of cast-on stitches dictates the length. The calculations here show the procedure for lengthening or shortening the back and front of such a sweater. The figures will of course vary in each case.

Total length of sleeve = 12⅜in (32cm)

Number of cast-on stitches for seam = 38 sts

Youn want to add 1¼in (3cm) in length.

Look at the stitch gauge; in this pattern it is 12 stitches to 4in (10cm) (i.e.) 3 stitches = 1in (1⅛ stitches = 1cm).

For an extra 1¼in (3cm) length, you need 3 stitches x 1¼ = 3¾ (4 stitches is nearest whole number)

Cast on (38 + 4) = 42 stitches in all.

4 The length of a sleeve worked from seam to seam also depends on the number of cast-on stitches. Add more or fewer stitches according to whether you want to lengthen or shorten the sleeve: follow the process shown in our example to see how to calculate this.

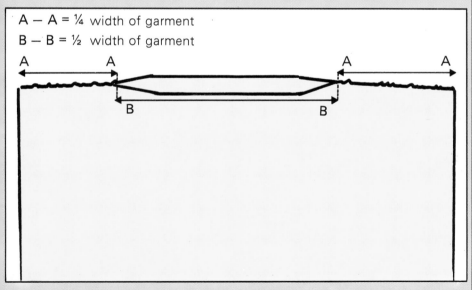

A — A = ¼ width of garment
B — B = ½ width of garment

5 The length of the neck opening can be varied again to suit individual requirements. Generally the neckline should be about half the width of the back or front. Join the shoulder seams for the same distance from each side edge, leaving an opening in the center large enough for the head to go through.

Planning your own design

The basic pattern pieces and measurements for the T-shaped sweater can easily be used as a basis for your own designs. You can choose different stitch patterns or change direction of knitting, but you must calculate the number of stitches to cast on. Don't assume, for example, that the number of stitches you cast on for the back of the garter-stitch sweater will be the same as the number you use for seed stitch; the finished piece of knitting will not be the correct size, since different stitch patterns and different yarns have widely varying gauges. You must always make a sample to test your gauge first and then work out the number of stitches to cast on.

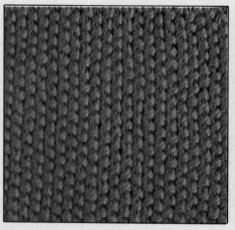

1 Choose the yarn and appropriate needles for that yarn. Make a gauge sample in the stitch pattern for the design. The sample shows a seed-stitch fabric knitted in a bulky yarn.

2 Measure the stitch gauge: here it is 15 stitches to 4in (10cm). The row gauge is unimportant if you are using the basic pattern pieces: you work to a given measurement rather than to a number of rows.

Fred Mancini

continued

3 Calculate the number of stitches to cast on. Suppose you are making the 26in (66cm) size sweater and want to knit the back from lower edge to top—follow the calculations shown in the diagram. Apply the same method to each piece of knitting.

Stitch gauge = 15 stitches to 4in (10cm)
Number of stitches to 1in = $3\frac{3}{4}$
Width of piece of knitting must be 14in (35cm)
Number of stitches to cast on = $3\frac{3}{4}$ stitches x 14 = $52\frac{1}{2}$ stitches
Cast on 53 stitches (the nearest whole number) to achieve the correct width

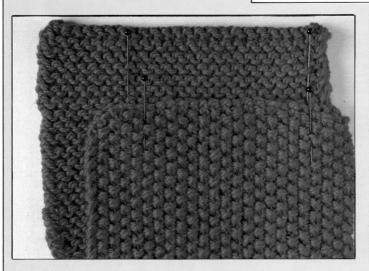

4 Don't assume that the same number of cast-on stitches necessarily works with a different stitch pattern, even if you use the same yarn and needles. Compare the width of 15 stitches in seed stitch with the same number in garter stitch. The difference is more pronounced with a greater number of stitches.

5 The calculation in step 3 applies to seed stitch in *bulky* yarn. If you decide on the same stitch but a different weight of yarn—say knitting worsted—you must make a gauge sample to find out the number of cast-on stitches. Note the difference between an equal number of stitches and rows in bulky yarn and knitting worsted yarn.

Single crochet edging

Give your T-shaped designs a touch of originality with various edgings or embroidery. Outline all the knitted pieces with crochet before joining them together, as in the garter-stitch sweater; or use crochet to finish outer edges after the garment is sewn up. You need no previous knowledge of crochet to attempt this edging and it is suitable for many knitted fabrics other than the garter-stitch one shown here. Choose a solid-color yarn to contrast with a tweedy or multi-colored fabric. Knitting worsted is a suitable weight for trimming bulky fabrics: use a medium-sized hook with this type of yarn. On our sweater there is some distance between the single crochet stitches; bridge the spaces with single chains. Some less bulky fabrics may not require extra stitches.

1 Hold the piece of knitting so that bound-off edge is at top. Insert crochet hook from front to back through knitting at right edge about $1\frac{1}{4}$in (3cm) from top.

2 Fold over end of yarn for crochet for about 4in (10cm): hold this folded end with your left hand. Insert crochet hook in the loop of yarn; draw the hook with the loop on it through to the front of the knitting.

3 Secure yarn by inserting hook from left to right under double strand of yarn at back of work. Draw strands of yarn through loop on hook.

4 Continue working with one strand of yarn from the ball, leaving the tail end free. It is easier to work if you wind the yarn around the fingers of your left hand as shown. Keep your left index finger flexible to control the yarn.

5 Insert hook from front to back under strand of yarn and draw through loop on hook; this is called one chain.

6 Insert hook from front to back through next stitch in knitting, about 1¼in (3cm) from top. Put hook under and over yarn at back of work and draw a loop through to the front: keep work relaxed and draw loop level with top edge of work.

7 Insert hook from front to back under strand of yarn and draw through both loops on the hook. One single crochet edge stitch is now complete.

8 Continue one single crochet edge stitch into each knitted stitch— with one chain between stitches—to within about one stitch of left edge.

9 To turn the corner, work one chain and one single crochet edge stitch, twice: insert hook each time into base of last stitch at left edge.

10 The side edge of the knitting now forms the top edge. Continue working edging as before, working about one single crochet edge stitch between garter-stitch ridges.

11 Work edging around sides as required. To finish off in this case, insert hook into first stitch worked and draw yarn through both loops on hook. Cut off yarn about 4in (10cm) from hook and draw cut end through loop on hook; pull end gently to secure loop.

Fred Mancini

Knitting for child's play

Have fun adapting this basic T-shaped top. We start the ball rolling with three simple but distinctive sweaters that show what can be done with this quick, easy shape.

Sizes

To fit 20[22:24:26:28:30]in (50[56:61:66:71:76]cm) chest: other measurements are shown on diagram. The figures in brackets [ ], refer to larger sizes.

Materials

Garter-stitch sweater *total of 20[22:22:23:25:25]oz (575[625:625:650:700:700]g) of bulky tweed-effect knitting yarn; scraps of knitting worsted*
1 pair No. 9 (6mm) knitting needles
Size H (5.00mm) crochet hook
Stockinette-stitch sweater *total of 11[11:13:13:15:15]oz (325[325:375:375:425:425]g) of bulky knitting yarn; scraps of contrasting bulky yarn for embroidery*
1 pair No. 6 (4½mm) knitting needles
Multi-stitch sweater *total of 8[11:11:13:13:15]oz (225[325:325:375:375:425]g) of bulky knitting yarn*
1 pair No. 6 (4½mm) knitting needles

Gauge

Garter-stitch sweater 12 sts and 24 rows to 4in (10cm) in garter st worked on No. 9 (6mm) needles.
Stockinette-stitch sweater and **Multi-stitch sweater** 15 sts and 22 rows to 4in (10in) in stockinette st worked on No. 6 (4½mm) needles.

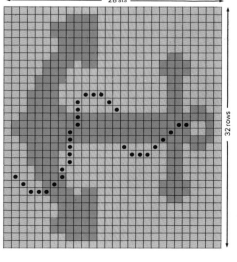

Rupert Watts

Frederick Verkroost

Garter-stitch sweater

Back and front (alike)
Using No. 9 (6mm) needles cast on 35[40:45:50:55:60:] sts for side edge.
Work in garter st for 11[11¾:13:13¾:15: 15¾]in (28[30:33:35:38:40]cm).

Sleeves
Using No. 9 (6mm) needles cast on 22[26:30:34:38:42] sts for seam.
Work in garter st for 8¼[9:10¼:11:12¼: 13]in (21[23:26:28:31:33]cm) from one seam to the other. Bind off.

To finish
Do not block.
Using size H (5.00mm) hook and contrasting yarn, work a single crochet edging all around back and front.
Work a similar edging along top and lower edge of sleeves (i.e. along row ends on sleeve pieces).
Join back and front at shoulders by overcasting, leaving about 6[6¼:6¾:7:7½: 8]in (15[16:17:18:19:20.5]cm) open.

Mark center of sleeve top edge with a pin: match pin to shoulder seam and overcast sleeves in position. Note that the wrong side of the single crochets at lower edge must be on the outside so that the cuff can be turned up on the right side.
Join side and sleeve seams (side seams by overcasting and sleeves with a backstitch seam), reversing seam at cuff edge. Leave slits in the side seams if desired.

Stockinette-stitch sweater

Back and front (alike)
Using No. 6 (4½mm) needles cast on
44[50:56:62:68:74] sts for side edge.
Work 4 rows garter st.
Beg with a K row and keeping 3 sts at
each end of row in garter st, cont in
stockinette st until work measures 10¼[11:
12¼:13:14¼:15]in (26[28:31:33:36.5:
38]cm) from beg, ending with a K row.
Work 4 rows garter st. Bind off.

Sleeves
Using No. 6 (4½mm) needles cast on
32[35:38:42:46:50] sts for wrist edge.
Work 4 rows in garter st.
Beg with a K row, continue in
stockinette st until work measures 6¼[7¾:
9:10½:11¾:13]in (16[19.5:23:27:30:
33]cm) ending with a K row.
Work 4 rows garter st. Bind off.

To finish
Block work but do not press borders.
Embroider anchor in duplicate stitch
and rope in chain stitch on front as shown
in diagram on page 51.
Join shoulder seams with a flat seam,
leaving approximately 6[6¼:6¾:7:7½:8]in
(15[16:17:18:19:20.5]cm) open for neck.
Mark center of bound-off sleeve edge
with a pin: match the pin to the shoulder
seam and sew in the sleeves with a flat
seam.
Join side and sleeve seams.

Multi-stitch sweater

Back and front (alike)
Using No. 6 (4½mm) needles cast on
44[48:56:60:68:72] sts. Work 1¼[2:2:2¾:
2¾:3½]in (3[5:5:7:7:9]cm) seed st.
Work 16 rows in K4, P4 basket st,
alternating blocks of stockinette st and
reverse stockinette st every 4 rows.
Beg first row (right side of work) with
K4, cont in K4, P4 ribbing until work
measures 8[8¾:10¼:11:12½:14¼]in
(20.5[22.5:26:28:32:36.5]cm) from
beg, ending with a wrong side row.
Beg next row with P4, work 16 rows
in K4, P4 basket st.
Work 1¼[2:2:2¾:2¾:3½]in (3[5:5:7:7:
9]cm) in seed st. Bind off loosely.

Sleeves
Using No. 6 (4½mm) needles cast on
28[32:36:40:44:48] sts for wrist edge.
Work 1¼[2:2:2¾:2¾:3½]in (3[5:5:7:7:
9]cm) in seed st.
Work 32[32:40:40:48:48] rows in K4,
P4 basket st.
Work 1¼[2:2:2¾:3½]in (3[5:5:7:7:
9]cm) in seed st. Bind off loosely.

To finish
Seed and basket st sections do not need
to be blocked: lightly press ribbed
section.
Complete in the same way as the
stockinette-stitch sweater but omit the
embroidery.

Sewing / COURSE 11

*Fitting problems with
set-in sleeves
*Slip stitch
*Attaching a double yoke
*Making a bias-cut tie
collar
*Pattern for a tie-neck blouse:
directions for making (1)

Fitting problems on a garment with set-in sleeves

Although some fitting adjustments can be made after a garment is cut out and basted together, it is often necessary to alter the pattern beforehand. This is particularly true in the case of shoulders and arms. You will know from past experience if you have a fitting problem in these areas, and if so, you should make the appropriate adjustments in the pattern before cutting out the garment. To make the correct alterations for the particular pattern, you should first cut out the main pattern pieces — bodice front and back, yoke (if any), and sleeve — in muslin and baste them together as directed in the pattern. Try on the muslin version (called a toile) and mark with pins or chalk the amounts by which the pattern pieces should be decreased or increased. (A dressmaker's dummy is a great help in doing this; if you don't have one, enlist the help of a friend or relative while you try the toile on yourself.) When necessary, remove the basting at seams and repin to let out extra fabric, or slash into the muslin and spread the pieces to achieve a smooth and comfortable fit. Make careful notes of the amounts to be taken in or out. Then, when you alter the paper pattern, you will know exactly where, and by how much, it should be altered.

Square shoulders

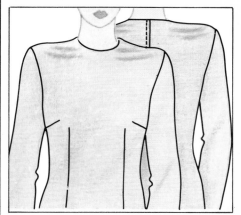
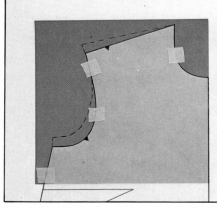
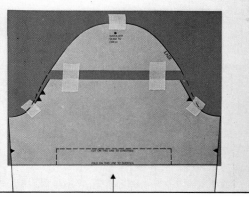

Square shoulders will cause wrinkles in the garment across the neckline. To correct this problem, tape a piece of paper behind the front and back bodice pieces. Draw and cut the new shoulder line, adding the required amount — between $\frac{1}{2}$ and $\frac{3}{4}$in (1.3 and 2cm)—at the shoulder and tapering to nothing at the neck. Raise the line at the underarm to maintain the original size of the armhole. In some cases, a square-shouldered figure may also require a larger armhole. If so, omit the addition at the underarm, but increase the depth of the sleeve cap, as shown, to make it fit into the larger armhole with the correct amount of ease at the same time allowing the greatest facility of movement.

Sloping shoulders

Sloping shoulders cause folds around the underarm. To correct the pattern, draw a new shoulder line below the edge of the pattern. At the armhole edge, measure the amount by which the shoulder line should be lowered (this may differ on the front and the back). Draw the line from this point, tapering up to nothing at the neck. Cut away the required amount. Cut away the same amount at the underarm to retain the original size.

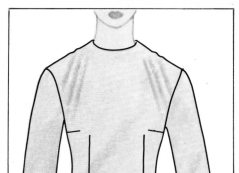
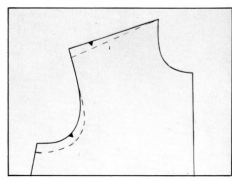

Terry Evans

Large upper arm

A large upper arm causes horizontal wrinkles in the sleeve. Slash the sleeve pattern vertically through the center, from the lower edge to the cap. Spread the pattern apart by the required amount and tape it to a piece of paper. Re-draw the lower edge of the sleeve and mark the grain line on the inserted piece of paper.

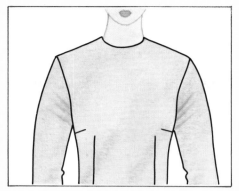

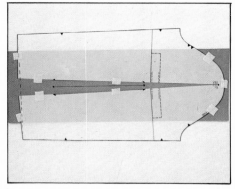

Slip stitch

Slip stitch is used for hems and for joining two pieces of fabric together. It should be virtually invisible.

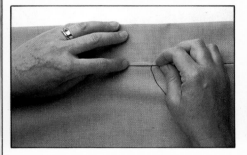

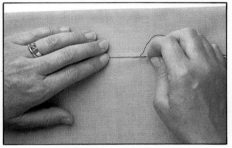

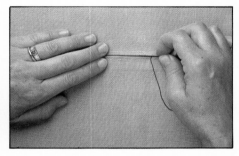

1 Work the stitch from right to left beginning with a double back stitch. Slide the needle along the hem fold and pick up $\frac{1}{8}$ to $\frac{1}{4}$ in (3 to 5mm).

2 Bring needle out and pick up one thread from the garment fabric. Insert needle into the fold where it came out and pick up another $\frac{1}{8}$ to $\frac{1}{4}$ in (3 to 5mm).

3 If joining two edges together, pick up an equal amount alternately from each edge.

Attaching a double yoke to a gathered bodice

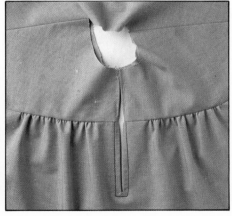

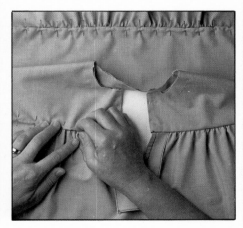

1 With right sides together and notches matching, pin the front and back yoke pieces to the front and back bodices, pulling up the bodice gathers to fit the yoke. Baste and stitch seams. Remove the gathering threads and press the seam allowance upward.

2 With right sides together and notches matching, baste and stitch the front and back yoke pieces together at the shoulders. Repeat this step on facings. Press all shoulder seams open. With right sides together, baste and stitch yoke facing to yoke at center front from yoke seam to neck edge. Turn to right side and baste close to stitched edges.

3 Turn under the seam allowance along the lower edges of the front and back yoke facings and baste along edges. With wrong sides together, matching neck and armhole edges, pin and baste the yoke facing to yoke at neck and armholes. On inside, pin and slip stitch the lower edges of the front and back yoke facings to the yoke stitching line.

Making a bias-cut tie collar

To obtain a smooth fit around the neck and a soft tie at the front, tie collars should be cut on the bias of the fabric. When the collar is cut on the bias it is more pliable; for this reason, you should be careful not to stretch it out of shape. A long tie collar may have to be cut in two pieces (depending on the width of the fabric) and joined with a seam at the center back, as shown in the photographs below.

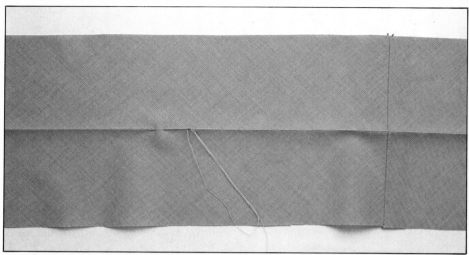

1 With right sides together and notches matching, baste and stitch the center back seam of the collar. Press seam open. Fold in half along length, wrong sides together. Press. Make a row of basting stitches along the foldline of the collar.

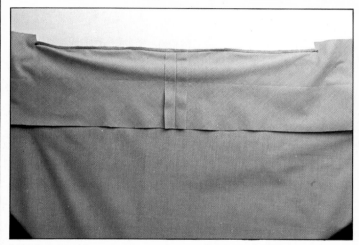

2 With right sides together and center backs and circles matching, pin and baste one edge of the collar to the neck edge. Stitch between circles. Grade seam allowances and press toward collar.

3 With right sides together fold tie ends in half lengthwise along the line of basting. Baste and stitch along edges to circles and across ends. Trim seam allowance and cut across corners.

4 Turn ties right side out and baste close to folded and stitched edges. Press.

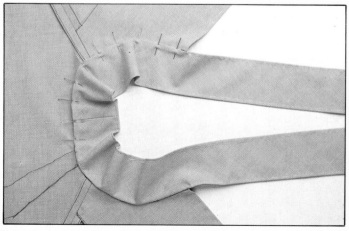

5 On the inside turn under the seam allowance of the free edge of the collar and slip stitch to neck seamline. Press.

Tie-neck blouse: directions for making (1)

Use the techniques in the course to make this elegant blouse. The soft neckline makes it perfect to wear with a suit. The directions will be completed in the next course.

Measurements

The pattern is given in sizes 10, 12, 14, 16, 18 and 20. Our pattern sizes correspond to sizes 8-18 in ready-made clothes and a guide to the size is on page 2.

Finished length from regular neckline;

(in)	24	24½	25	25½	26	26½
(cm)	61	62.5	63.5	65	66	67.5

Suggested fabrics

The blouse shown is made in a satin-finish rayon. Use a fabric which drapes well, such as a light jersey, fine wool/cotton blend or crepe fabric.

Materials

36in (90cm)-wide fabric with or without nap
Sizes   10, 12, 14: 3⅛yd (2.9m)
        16, 18, 20: 3¼yd (3m)
45in (115cm)-wide fabric with or without nap
Sizes   10, 12: 2⅞yd (2.6m)
        14, 16: 3yd (2.7m)
        18, 20: 3⅛yd (2.8m)
54in (140cm)-wide fabric with or without nap
Sizes   10, 12, 14: 2⅛yd (1.9m)
        16, 18, 20: 2¼yd (2m)
¼yd (.2m) of 36in (90cm)-wide interfacing

John Carter

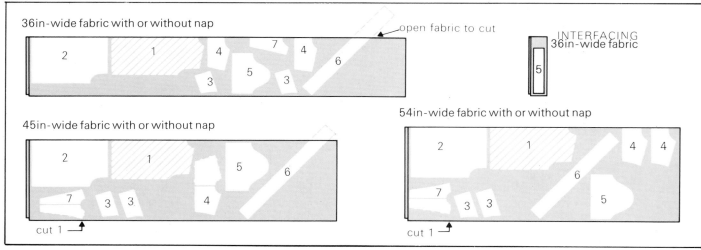

Key to pattern pieces

1	Blouse front	Cut 1 on fold
2	Blouse back	Cut 1 on fold
3	Front yoke and yoke facing	Cut 4
4	Back yoke and yoke facing	Cut 2 on fold
5	Sleeve and cuff	Cut 2
6	Neck tie	Cut 2
7	Front facing	Cut 1 on fold

Use piece 5 (between fold line and inner fold line) for interfacing.

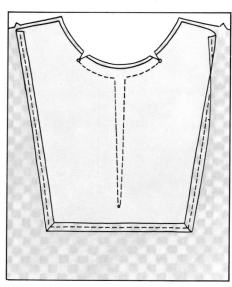

1 Finish the outer edge of the center front facing by turning under $\frac{1}{4}$in (5mm) and stitching. Press. With right sides together and circles and center fronts matching, baste facing to blouse front. Stitch along seamline from circle at neck edge to within $\frac{1}{4}$in (5mm) of the center front. Continue stitching along opening, tapering to the point at center front circle. Take an extra stitch across the bottom of the opening and continue stitching up the other side and across neck edge to circle. Clip seam to circle.

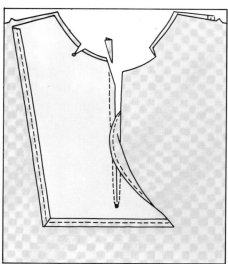

2 Slash between stitching to point. Cut across corners. Turn facing to inside and baste around opening. Press.

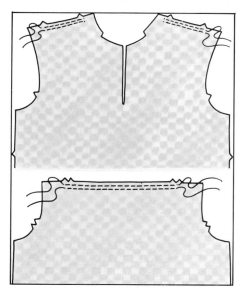

3 Press two rows of gathering stitches between notches on the front and back blouse prices.

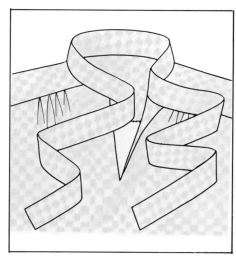

4 Apply the front and back yokes and yoke facings to the bodice. Apply the tie collar to the neck edge.

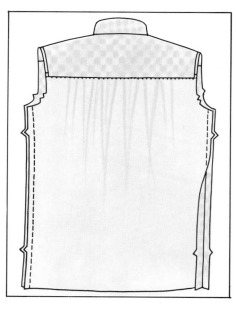

5 With right sides together and notches matching, baste and stitch the side seams. Finish the seams and press open.

Sewing/COURSE 12

*Setting in sleeves
*Pattern for a tie-neck blouse:
 directions for making (2)

Setting in sleeves

All set-in sleeves are cut with a sleeve cap that is larger than the armhole into which it fits. The extra fullness — called "ease" — enables the sleeve to fit over the rounded shape of the arm and hang correctly; it also allows freedom of movement. The fullness must be distributed evenly over the sleeve, but the cap must not appear to be gathered. Ripples around the top of a sleeve are one sign of a home-made garment. When using some crisp fabrics you may find it difficult to distribute the ease evenly. In this case, run the gathering threads about ¾in (2cm) past the notches on each side, so that the fullness is distributed evenly over a larger area.

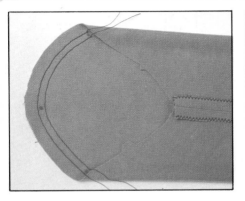

1 To prepare the sleeve cap for easing, run two rows of gathering stitches around the upper edge between the notches ⅛in (3mm) to each side of the seamline. Stitch the underarm sleeve seam, press open and finish raw edges. Turn sleeve right side out.

2 With right sides together, underarm seams and notches matching and circle to shoulder seam, pin sleeve into armhole. Pull up the gathering threads, working on the two ends alternately, to ease in the fullness until the sleeve fits the armhole. Baste, spreading the gathers evenly. For greater control of the ease, leave the pins in until the sleeve is machine stitched in place.

3 Stitch the sleeve into the armhole, working with the sleeve on top. Add a second row of stitching, within the seam allowance, ¼in (5mm) from the first row. Remove the pins, basting and gathering threads.

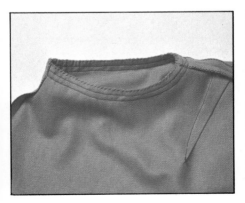

4 Do not trim the seam allowance but finish the raw edges together with hand overcasting. Clip the underarm curves.

5 Press the sleeve and armhole seams together, working on the sleeve side. This method prevents a ridge showing on the right side of the garment, as may happen if the seam is pressed toward the sleeve. When the garment is turned right side out, the seam allowance lies toward the sleeve.

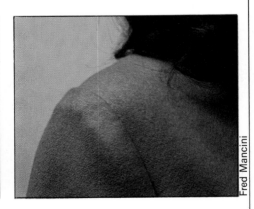

6 the finished sleeve should fit smoothly over the shoulder edge, with no tucks or gathers in the seam.

Fred Mancini

Tie-neck blouse directions for making (2):

Simple seaming and a gathered yoke-line give an up-to-date look to this classic style. The tie neck is loosely bowed and falls centrally over the front fastening. Make it in crisp cotton for summer wear, fine wool to go under a jacket in winter or in stunning satin for evening. For the first part of these directions, see Sewing Course 11, page 57.

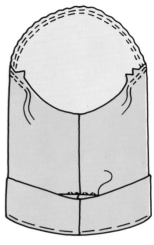

5 On the right side, topstitch along the top edge of cuff, stitching $\frac{1}{4}$in (5mm) in from the folded edge. Catch-stitch the cuff to sleeve at the underarm seam.

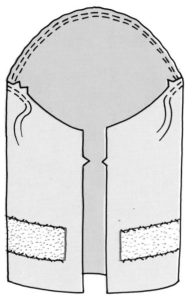

1 Prepare the sleeve cap for easing by working two lines of gathering stitches. Baste interfacing to wrong side of sleeve between inner foldline and foldline. Catch-stitch to both foldlines.

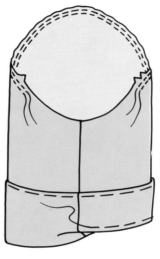

3 Working on the right side, fold the cuff into position, folding along the inner foldline (bottom of cuff) and foldline (top of cuff). Baste along the foldline edge. Press. Turn the hem allowance to the inside of sleeve, folding along the inner foldline. Baste close to lower edge.

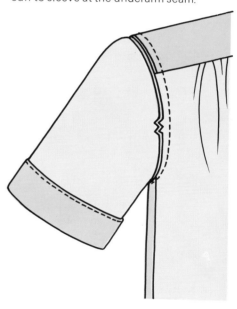

6 With right sides together, matching underarm seams, notches and circle to shoulder seam, pin, baste and stitch sleeve to armhole, distributing ease evenly. Press the seam allowance and finish raw edges. Repeat steps 1 through 6 for second sleeve.

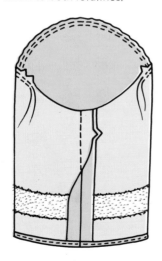

2 With right sides together and notches matching, baste and stitch the underarm seam of sleeve. Trim the interfacing close to the stitching. Finish seam allowances and press seam open. Finish the lower edge of sleeve by turning under $\frac{1}{4}$in (5mm) and stitching.

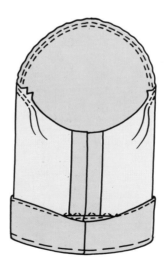

4 On the inside sew hem to sleeve using a catch-stitch. Make sure that the stitches do not show on the right side. Press cuff into place; turn sleeve right side out. Remove top row of basting and re-press so that the basting marks do not show.

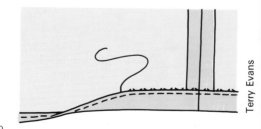

7 Turn under the raw edge along the lower edge of the blouse and stitch close to edge. Trim. Turn under $\frac{1}{4}$in (5mm), hem by hand and press.

Terry Evans

pattern pack

*Fitting problems on an
 A-line skirt
*Hem finished with straight
 seam binding
*Pattern for an A-line skirt:
 directions for making

Fitting a flared skirt is relatively easy. When you buy a skirt pattern you should buy the size corresponding to your hip measurement (taken at a point 8in [20cm] down from your waist). Also use this measurement in choosing the cutting line for the A-line skirt in the Pattern Pack. If your waist is smaller than that indicated for your size, take in the excess fabric in seams and darts. You may find that other problems may require adjusting the pattern to your figure.

Fitting problems on an A-skirt

Large seat

1 This will cause the skirt to wrinkle across the back and ride up. The width and the length of the skirt must be increased at the fullest part of the seat.

2 Determine the amount of adjustment by measuring across the fullest part of the seat from one side to the other. Then compare this measurement with the width (doubled) of the back pattern piece. Remember to allow about $\frac{3}{4}$–2in (2–5cm) for ease.

3 Slash the pattern vertically through the center of the back waist dart. Slash the pattern horizontally about 8in [20cm] below the waistline, from the center back through the side seam. Spread the vertical slash apart by one quarter of the amount to be increased. Tape the pieces in place over a sheet of paper. Spread the horizontal slash by the same amount, keeping the center back straight. Tape in place. The back is now longer than the front, so take the additional amount off the hem at the side seam tapering to nothing at the center back. Adjust the dart length to correspond to the fullest part of the figure. Re-draw the cutting lines at side and back edges.

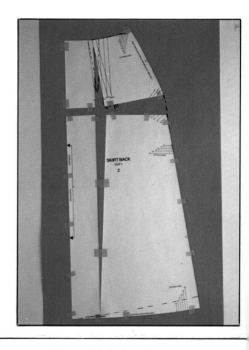

Small seat

1 If the seat is small, the skirt falls in folds across the back and tends to sag. The width and length of the skirt must be decreased at the fullest part of the seat.

2 Determine the amount of adjustment in the same way as for a large seat. Draw a line at right angles to the grain line 4in (10cm) below the waist. Slash this line to the side seam. Lap the lower sections over the upper section by the necessary amount at the center back, tapering to nothing at the side. Re-draw the center back to make it straight, following the original edge. Re-draw hem, tapering the line to meet original hemline at the side.

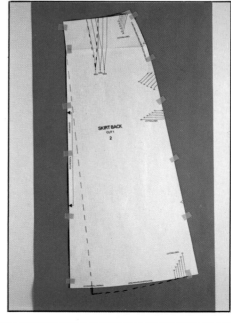

Terry Evans

Large abdomen

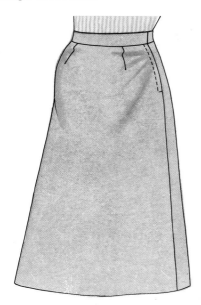

1 If the abdomen is large, the skirt will be tight over this area. The width of the skirt must be increased below the waist. Extra length is also needed in the abdomen area.

2 Determine the amount of increase by measuring over the fullest part of the abdomen from side to side and comparing this measurement with that of the front pattern piece, allowing for the dart, if any, and for ease.

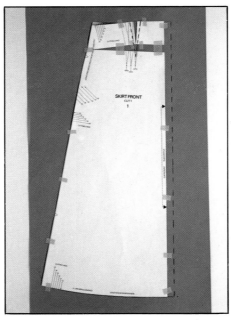

3 Draw a line through the waist dart. Draw a horizontal line about 2¾in (7cm) below the waist. Slash through the dart to the line. Slash along the horizontal line to the side seam. Spread the horizontal slash by one-quarter of the required amount, and the dart slash also by one-quarter of the amount, keeping the center front straight. Tape in place over paper. Re-draw the waist dart. If extra width is needed, add at front.

Sway back

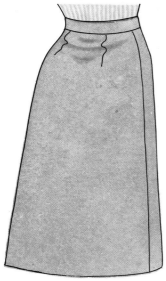

1 This causes wrinkles below the back waist. This alteration can be done at the fitting stage if you prefer.

2 If you are altering the pattern, use the method described for altering pants in Volume 2, page 59.

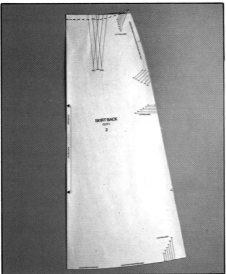

3 If you are making the alteration on the skirt itself, pin out the extra fullness across the back of the skirt, making a horizontal dart. Take off the skirt and measure the amount taken up by the dart. Cut this amount off the top edge of the skirt, tapering to the waistline at the side edge.

Hem finished with straight seam binding

This method for turning up a hem is used on fabrics that ravel, or on thick fabrics where bulk must be avoided. It also makes a neat finish for unlined garments. After the hem has been turned up, basted, and an even width of hem allowance marked, the straight binding is applied. Bias binding should not be used for this type of hem, since it will stretch in wear and will cause unsightly dragging.

1 After marking the hemline and before turning up the hem, cut a notch into the seam allowances at the hem fold line. This will reduce the bulk on the fold line, making the hem lie flatter at this point. If using a thick fabric, you can further reduce the bulk at the hemline by trimming the seam allowance away on the hem allowance only.

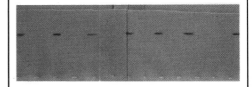

2 Turn up and baste hem close to folded edge. Using tailor's chalk, mark the hem allowance.

3 With the right side of the hem allowance on top, place the binding on the marked hem width line. Baste and stitch the binding to the right side of the hem allowance, stitching close to tape edge. Where the ends of the tape meet, turn under ⅜in (1cm) at one end; lap it over the other. Trim any extra hem allowance so that none extends above binding.

4 Using hemming stitch, sew the free edge of the binding to the skirt, taking care not to pull the stitches too tightly.

Paul Williams

A-line skirt: directions for making

Easy to make and wonderfully versatile

Measurements
The pattern is given in sizes 10, 12, 14, 16, 18 and 20, corresponding to sizes 8-18 in ready-made clothes. A guide to our sizes appears on page 2. The finished lengths from natural waistline: $28\frac{1}{2}$, 29, $29\frac{1}{2}$, 30, $30\frac{1}{2}$, 31 in (72.5, 73.5, 75, 76.5, 78, 78.5cm).

Suggested fabrics
Medium-weight woolens such as flannel and gaberdine, linen or synthetic linen weaves, corduroy.

Materials
36in (90cm)-wide fabric without nap:
Sizes 10, 12: $2\frac{1}{8}$yd (1.9m)
Sizes, 14, 16, 18, 20: $3\frac{3}{8}$yd (2.1m)

45in (115cm) and 54in (140cm)
fabric with or without nap:
Sizes 10, 12, 14, 16, 18: $2\frac{1}{8}$yd (1.9m)
Size 20: $2\frac{1}{4}$yd (2m)

36in (90cm)-wide interfacing fabric:
Sizes 10, 12, 14, 16, 18: $\frac{1}{4}$yd (15cm)
Size 20: $\frac{3}{8}$yd (25cm)
Matching thread
7in (18cm) skirt zipper
Skirt hook and eye

Key to pattern pieces
1	Skirt front	Cut 1 on fold
2	Skirt back	Cut 1 on fold
3	Waistband	Cut 1

Interfacing
Use piece 3.

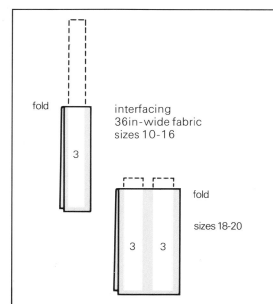

interfacing
36in-wide fabric
sizes 10-16

fold

sizes 18-20

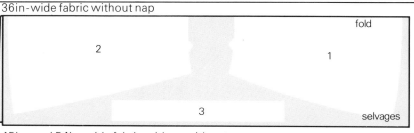
36in-wide fabric without nap

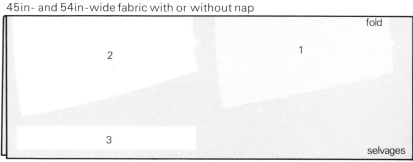
45in- and 54in-wide fabric with or without nap

Cutting out

1 Cut out the pattern pieces on the pattern sheet following the correct line for the size you want.
2 Prepare the fabric and pin on the pattern pieces, following the layouts given on page 64. Make sure you place the pieces with the direction lines on the correct grain of the fabric. Cut out the garment.
3 Transfer all pattern markings.

Fitting

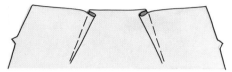

1 Baste the front and back waist darts.

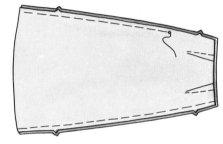

2 With right sides together, matching notches, baste the front and back skirt pieces together at the side seams, joining the left side seam up to the circle only. Baste the zipper into the left opening.

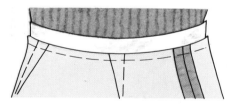

3 Baste the skirt to a temporary waistband. Cut one of these from a length of grosgrain ribbon, which can be kept for future use.

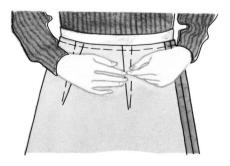

4 Try on skirt and pin out any alterations, distributing the amounts evenly. Mark the alterations with tailor's chalk or basting stitches. Remove temporary waistband and zipper.

Completing

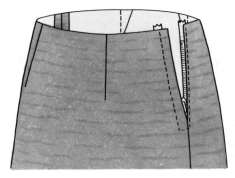

1 Stitch the front and back waist darts and side seams, stitching the left side seam to circle. Press darts toward center and press seams open. Finish raw edges. Insert the zipper into the left side using the lapped seam method.

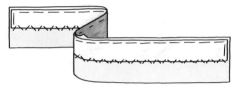

2 For the larger size join the two interfacing pieces before stitching to waistband. Baste interfacing to the wrong side along notched edge of the side of the waistband along notched edge. Catch-stitch interfacing to foldline.

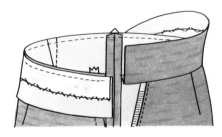

3 With right sides together and waistband notch at right side seam, baste and stitch the waistband to skirt. Trim interfacing close to stitching. Grade seam allowance and press toward waistband.

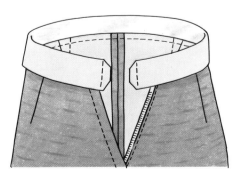

4 With right sides together, fold waistband along foldline. Baste and stitch across ends. Trim interfacing and cut across corners.

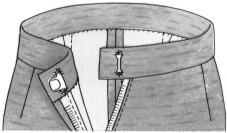

5 Turn the waistband right side out and baste folded edge. On the inside turn under the seam allowance of the waistband and hem to stitching line. Press. Sew skirt hook and eye to waistband.

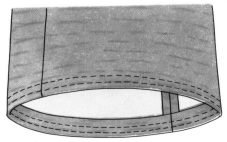

6 Turn the hem up using the straight binding method. Then, working on the right side, add a row of topstitching $\frac{1}{4}$in (5mm) from the lower edge and a second row $\frac{3}{4}$in (2cm) above the first. Press finished skirt.

Sewing/COURSE 14

*More fitting problems
*Using interfacing
*Pattern for a short-sleeved
 jacket: directions for making
 (1)

More fitting problems

Locating the bust point

The bust area of a garment should fit smoothly, and there should be enough ease for comfortable movement. The waist and bust darts should point to the fullest part of the bust — called the bust point. If the garment does not fit smoothly it is possible that the bust is high or low in relation to the pattern.

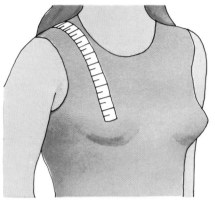

1 To determine whether the bust is high or low, measure from the middle of your shoulder to the tip of the bust.

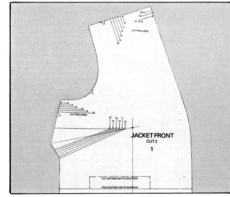

2 On the pattern, draw intersecting lines through the bust and waist darts to locate the bust point.

High bust

If the bust is high, the bodice fullness will fall below the bust, causing pulling across the actual bustline. In this case, the bust dart must be raised and the waist dart extended upwards.

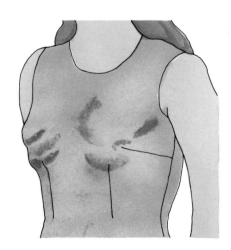

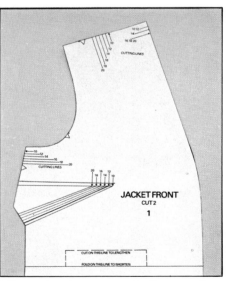

1 Determine the amount of adjustment by comparing the actual measurement to bust point with the measurement on the pattern. Measure up from the original bust dart point on the pattern and mark this new point. Raise each of the dart lines by this amount at the side seam. Re-draw the bust dart lines in their new positions, the new dart lines being parallel to the original lines. Raise the point of the waist dart by the same amount.

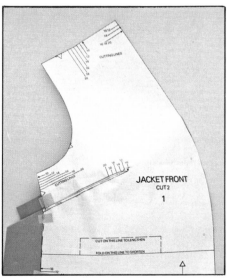

2 To obtain the correct shape of the new bust dart at the side seam, tape a piece of paper underneath the side seam edge. Fold the new dart and pin it in place. Cut along the side cutting line, tapering to the waistline. Remove pins and open out dart.

Low bust

If the bust is low, the fullness will fall above the bustline, causing pulling across the actual bustline. The bust darts must be lowered and the point of the waist darts moved downward.

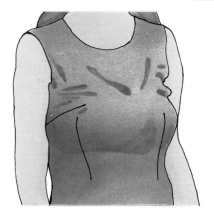

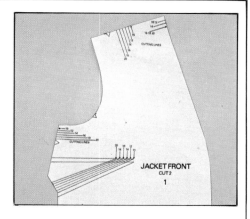

1 Determine the amount of adjustment by comparing the actual measurement to bust point with the measurement on the pattern. Measure down from the original dart point on the pattern and mark this new point. Draw a new dart in the new

position, as for a high bust, step 1. Lower the point of the waist dart by the same amount as you have lowered the bust dart. To obtain the correct shape of the new dart at the side seam, follow step 2 as for a high bust.

Round shoulders

If the shoulders are rounded, the bodice will wrinkle and pull from the back neckline toward the shoulders. This means that more length is required at the center back.

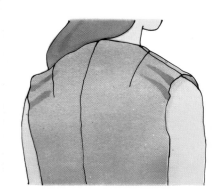

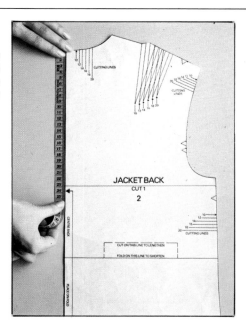

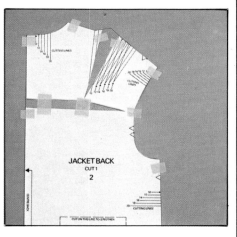

1 To determine the extra length needed, draw a **horizontal** line on the pattern from the center back to the underarm seamline. Enlist the help of a friend or relative to measure from your neck bone at center back down your spine to a point level with your underarm. Compare this measurement with the pattern from neck seamline to the horizontal line. The difference between the two measurements is the extra length needed. Slash the pattern horizontally at a point about 5in (12.5cm) down from the neck, from the center back to the armhole seamline—**not** to the armhole edge.

2 Slash down through the center of the shoulder dart to within $\frac{1}{4}$in (5mm) of the first slash. Raise the back neck and spread the shoulder to make a larger dart. Tape in place on a sheet of paper. Use the original dart stitching line when stitching the dart. To obtain the new shoulder line, draw new lines tapering from neck to original dart line and from shoulder to original dart line. If there is no shoulder dart, slash down at the center of the shoulder line to within $\frac{1}{4}$in (5mm) of the existing slash. Raise the back neck and spread the shoulder to make a dart. Tape in place on a sheet of paper.

3 To position dart point, measure down $4\frac{1}{2}$in (11.5cm) from the shoulder cutting line in the center of the slash. Draw the new dart tapering from either side of slash at the shoulder seamline to the dart point.

4 To make the new cutting line for the dart at the shoulder line, fold the dart and pin it in place. Cut along the shoulder cutting line from shoulder point to neck. Remove pins and open out dart.

Paul Williams

Broad back

A broad back will cause the bodice to pull across the back, restricting movement. The width of the back must be increased to allow the bodice to lie smoothly.

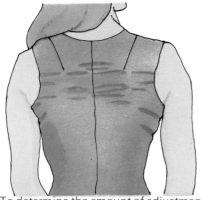

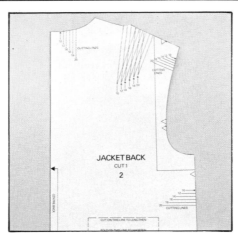

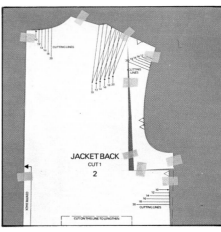

1 To determine the amount of adjustment, first measure across the back from armhole to armhole. Add 1in (2.5cm) ease allowance to this measurement; divide the total by two and compare this measurement with the measurement across the back bodice pattern piece from center back to seamline at underarm.

2 Draw a line across the bodice below the armhole. Draw a vertical line up to the shoulder seamline—**not** to the edge— approximately 1¼in (3cm) in from the armhole edge.

3 Slash along both lines, up to the shoulder seamline. Spread the vertical slash by the required amount of adjustment and tape in place on a sheet of paper. Re-draw the side seamline, tapering to the waistline. The side seam has now been increased in length. Lengthen the front side seam at the lower edge to match, or trim away the extra amount from the back, tapering to center front or center back as the case may be.

Using interfacing

Interfacing is fabric sometimes used between the main fabric and a facing in order to reinforce and add firmness to certain areas of a garment. It is often used at an edge, where it helps retain the shape of the garment in wear, and also in collars, cuffs, lapels, belts, waistbands and necklines. It must always be used on an area on which buttons or buttonholes are to be placed. Usually pattern directions indicate where interfacing is required.

Interfacing comes in various weights and types for use with different fabrics. The interfacing must be of the same or similar fiber content as the garment fabric; for example, linen or cotton interfacing is used with linen, cotton interfacing with cotton or woolens, rayon with rayon or other synthetics and silk. If the garment is to be washed, the interfacing must also be washable.

To interface medium-weight woolens and synthetics, or to give a crisp effect to firm cottons and linens, use medium-weight rayon or cotton, non-woven sew-on, or iron-on, or woven iron-on interfacing.

To give soft shaping to medium-weight fabrics or to give crisp shaping to sheers and laces, use lightweight cotton or rayon, woven iron-on interfacing or net, organdy, organza or lawn.

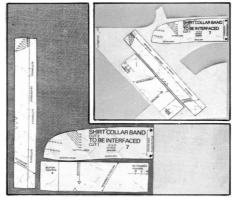

1 When using woven interfacing, lay the pattern piece on the correct grain line, as you would when cutting out ordinary woven dress fabric.

2 Non-woven interfacings do not have any grain, so the pattern pieces may be cut lying in any direction, making the most economical use of the fabric.

3 Trim down the inner unnotched edge of the interfacing, enough to prevent its showing beyond the facing edge. The amount you need to trim away will depend on the method of finishing to be used on the raw edge of the facing. For example, if you are turning in the raw edge by ¼in (5mm) and stitching, trim ⅜in (1cm) off the interfacing.

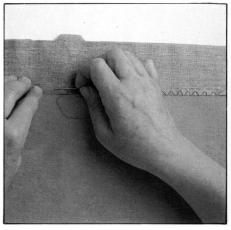

4 Lay the interfacing on the wrong side of the garment section, matching any notches and having raw edges even. Pin and baste in place. Catch-stitch the inner unnotched edge to the garment. If the outer edge of the interfacing is placed on a foldline and not included in a seam, catch-stitch this edge to the foldline.

5 Sew the garment together and prepare the facing for application. With right sides together and notches and seams matching, baste and stitch the facing to the garment. Trim the interfacing close to the seamline and grade the seam allowance.

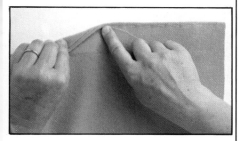

6 Turn the facing to the inside of the garment and with the right side of the garment uppermost, baste close to the stitched edge. To give a good smooth edge, roll the seam very slightly to the wrong side as you baste. Do not roll it too much or you will lose the crisp shaping.

This trim jacket looks stunning made in a variety of fabrics. Here it is in lightweight wool, equally suited to a fine spring day or a fall evening. In Sewing Course 15, Volume 4, page 57 we show you how to complete it.

Measurements
The pattern is given in sizes 10, 12, 14, 16, 18 and 20; corresponding to sizes 8-18 in ready-made clothes.

Suggested fabrics
The jacket should be made from a fabric with plenty of body. If you are not a very experienced dressmaker, use linen, denim or heavyweight cotton.

36in-wide fabric with or without nap

Cutting layouts

36in-wide interfacing

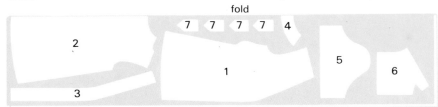

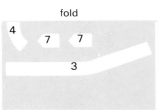

45in-wide fabric without nap

54in-wide fabric without nap

Materials

*36in (90cm)-wide fabric with or
  without nap
Sizes 10 and 12: 2½yd (2.3m)
Sizes 14 and 16: 2⅝yd (2.4m)
Sizes 18 and 20: 2⅞yd (2.6m)*

*45in (115cm)-wide fabric without nap
Sizes 10, 12, 14 and 16: 2⅛yd (1.9m)
Sizes 18 and 20: 2¼yd (2m)*

*54in (140cm)-wide fabric without nap
Sizes 10 and 12: 2yd (1.8m)
Sizes 14, 16, 18 and 20: 2⅛yd (1.9m)*

*36in (90cm)-wide woven interfacing
  for all sizes: 1⅛yd (1m)
Matching thread
Four ½in (1.3cm) buttons
Bias binding: seam binding*

Key to pattern pieces

1	Jacket front	Cut 2
2	Jacket back	Cut 1 on fold
3	Front facing	Cut 2
4	Back neck facing	Cut 1 on fold
5	Sleeve	Cut 2
6	Pocket	Cut 2
7	Tab	Cut 8

Interfacing: use pieces 3, 4 and 7

Cutting out

Cut out the pattern pieces from the pattern
sheet following the correct line for the size
you want. Prepare the fabric and pin on
the pattern pieces, following the layouts
on this page. Make sure you place pieces
with direction lines on the correct grain of
the fabric. Cut out the fabric following
closely the edges of the pattern pieces.
Transfer all pattern markings to the fabric
(see Volume 1, page 53).

Fitting and interfacing

1 Pin and baste the bust and shoulder
darts and the shoulder and side seams.
2 Try on the jacket and pin and mark any
fitting adjustments on the garment.
3 Remove basting from shoulder and side
seams and darts. Press all pieces flat on
wrong side.

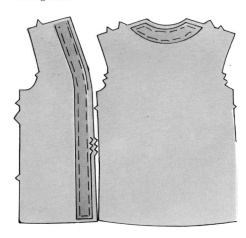

4 Baste the interfacing firmly to the wrong
side of the jacket front, neck edge and
back neck edge.

Stitching

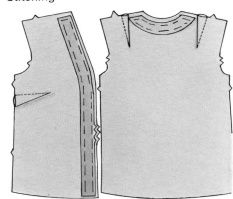

1 With right sides together, fold, pin,
baste and stitch the bust and back
shoulder darts. Press the bust darts
downward and the shoulder darts
toward the center back.

2 With right sides together and notches
matching, pin, baste and stitch the
shoulder seams and the side seams. Press
seams open and finish raw edges by hand
or machine overcasting.

Needlework / COURSE 5

*Materials for cross-stitch
 embroidery
*Cross-stitch
*Making a sampler

Cross-stitch embroidery

Many years ago, youg girls practiced their needlework as well as their letters and numbers by making cross-stitch samplers. Samplers are still popular, but cross-stitch is also widely used to decorate tablecloths and napkins, guest towels and clothing.

Cross-stitch is a form of counted thread embroidery — each stitch covers a specific number of horizontal and vertical threads of an evenly woven background fabric. The stitch is easy and simple designs can be worked quickly from a graph.

Materials

The best background fabrics for cross-stitch are medium-weight linens and cottons which have approximately 18 to 22 threads per inch (7 to 9 threads per cm), but any evenly woven fabric in which the threads are easy to see can be used.

The weight of the embroidery thread should be appropriate to the weight of the fabric. Thread that is too heavy will pucker the fabric, while thread that is too fine will not show up on the fabric or will break.

The most popular threads for cross-stitch are cotton for light- and medium-weight

Fabric, thread and needles for cross-stitch embroidery		
Even-weave fabric	Thread	Needle
Fine	1-6 strands embroidery floss pearl cotton	tapestry 20-24
Medium	3-6 strands embroidery floss pearl cotton 1 strand Persian wool crewel wool	tapestry 18-24
Coarse	6 or more strands embroidery floss 2 strands pearl cotton 2-3 strands Persian wool 2 or more strands crewel tapestry wool	tapestry 14-22

fabrics and wool for coarse fabrics. Cotton threads include six-strand embroidery floss and pearl cotton. Embroidery floss can be divided into strands and used in any thickness. Pearl cotton, which is more lustrous, is used whole but comes in several weights and can be doubled.

The main wool threads are Persian, tapestry and crewel. Persian can be separated into strands while tapestry is

usually used whole, Crewel, a thinner thread, can be used singly or doubled or tripled.

In cross-stitch, a tapestry needle is always used because its blunt end slips between the threads of the fabric. A general guide to fabrics, threads and needles is given in the chart on this page. Remember, however, that you may always use thicker or thinner threads in small areas for special effects.

Cross-stitch

The cross-stitch is a simple X formed by two overlapping straight stitches. The top stitch of every X should slant in the same direction. For this reason, embroiderers often stitch a whole row of lower stitches and then return along the same row adding the upper stitches as shown at right. If this is not practical, complete each stitch individually. When crosses are next to each other, their edges should share the same holes. Be sure that each cross covers the correct number of fabric threads and that every cross is aligned horizontally and vertically with the other crosses. Begin and end each embroidery thread with a small back stitch into the back of another stitch or use a tiny knot. Threads may be carried short distances across the back of the work.

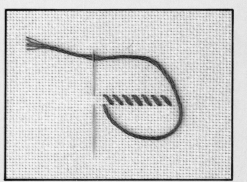

1 Bring needle up at lower right-hand corner of first cross. Insert it at upper left-hand corner and bring it up below at lower right-hand corner of second cross. Continue working from right to left to complete a row of half crosses.

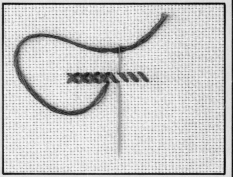

2 To finish the crosses, bring the needle up at the lower left-hand corner of the last cross. Insert it at the upper right-hand corner and bring it up below at the lower left-hand corner of the next cross.

Simon Butcher

Rainbow sampler

Learn to cross-stitch this bold alphabet sampler. Then use your skill to decorate everything from napkins to night gowns.

Size: embroidered area 9¾in (25cm) across; 12⅞in (33cm) deep.
Note: We embroidered our sampler on an even-weave linen with 22 threads to the inch (2.5cm). Each stitch covers 3 threads horizontally and vertically, giving us slightly more than 7 stitches to the inch (2.5cm). The size of your sampler will depend on the thread count of the material you use and the size of your stitches.

Materials

A rectangle of even-weave linen 3-4in (7.5-10cm) larger all around then the area to be embroidered
No. 22 tapestry needle
1-2 skeins embroidery floss each in blue, orange, purple, yellow and red (we used 1 skein each for our sampler; if yours will be larger, you may need 2)
3 skeins embroidery floss in green
Embroidery hoop or frame (optional)

To make

1 Cut the linen to the appropriate size (ours is 16×20in [41×51cm]).
2 Find the center of the linen by folding it crosswise and lengthwise. Mark the thread where the folds meet with a pin.
3 Count the number of graph squares included in the design from side edge to side edge. Multiply this figure by the number of threads each stitch is to cover (3 in our sampler). Divide this total by 2 to get half. Then count this number of threads from the center out to each side of the linen and mark with a pin. These are the side edges of the area to be embroidered.
4 Following the same procedure as in step 3, mark the upper and lower edges of the area to be embroidered.

5 Baste around the edges of the embroidery area following the threads marked at the sides, top and bottom. You may also mark the center with a thread.
6 To make the work easier and keep the fabric from being pulled by the stitches, you may mount it tightly in a frame.
7 Cut a length of yellow embroidery floss about 18in (46cm) long and thread all 6 strands through the tapestry needle.
8 Stitch the outer border first starting in the center at the top and working out to one side first, then the other. Then complete the sides and bottom. Complete inner border next, then alphabet, flower basket and butterflies.
9 Secure each end of each thread with a tiny back stitch into the back of an existing stitch or into the linen in an area where it will be covered by a stitch. Be careful not to pull thread too tight or it will distort the fabric.
10 Press the borders. If necessary to press the stitched area, place it face down on a folded towel or soft blanket and press with a cool iron and a press cloth.

CROCHET

And so to bed . . .

Bulky yarn worked in doubles makes cozy children's bathrobes to keep them warm while they watch that extra half hour of television or listen to a favorite bedtime story. Contrasting edging and belts add extra style.

Serge Krouglikoff

Sizes

To fit 24 [26:28:30]in (66[:71:76]cm) chest.
Length, boy's 26¾[28½:30½:32½]in (66[71:76:81]cm).
Length, girl's 30¼[32½:34½:36½]in (76[81:86:91]cm).
Sleeve seam, 10[12:14:16]in (25[30:35:40]cm).

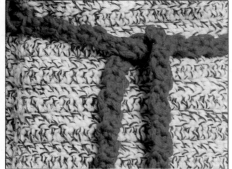

Note Directions for larger sizes are in brackets []; where there is only one set of figures it applies to all sizes.

Materials

Boy's bathrobe: *32[36:39:43]oz (900[1000:1100:1200]g) of a bulky yarn in main color (A) and 9[9:11:11]oz (250[250:300:300]g) in contrasting color (B)*
Girl's bathrobe: *41[44:48:52]oz (1150[1250:1350:1450]g) of a bulky yarn in main color (A) and 11[11:13:13]oz (300[300:350:350]g) in contrasting color (B)*
Sizes F, H and I (4.00, 5.00 and 6.00mm) hooks
For knitted belt, a pair of No. 6 (4½mm) needles

Gauge

11dc and 7 rows to 4in (10cm) worked on size I (6.00mm) hook.

Back

Using size I (6.00mm) hook and A, make 48[51:54:57] ch.
Base row 1dc into 4th ch from hook, 1dc into each ch to end. Turn. 46[49:52:55] sts.
1st row 3ch, skip first dc, 1dc into each dc to end, 1dc into top of turning ch. Turn.

Rep last row 5[7:9:9] times more.
Dec row 3ch, 1dc into each of next 14[15:16:17] dc, leaving last loop of each on hook, work 1dc into each of next 2dc, yo and draw through all loops on hook (1dc decreased), 1dc into each dc to within last 17[18:19:20] sts, dec 1dc, 1dc into each dc to end, 1dc into top of turning ch. Turn.
Work 7[9:11:11] rows without shaping.
Rep last 8[10:12:12] rows once more, then work the dec row again.
40[43:46:49] sts. Cont without shaping until work measures 20[21:22½:24]in (50[53:57:61]cm) from beg for boy's robe or 23½[25:26½:28]in (60[63:67:71]cm) from beg for girl's.
Shape raglan armholes
1st row Sl st into first 3 sts, 3ch, 1dc into each dc to within last 2 sts. Turn.
2nd row 3ch, skip first dc, dec 1dc, 1d into each dc to within last 3 sts, dec 1dc, 1dc into top of the turning ch. Turn.
Rep the last row until 16[17:18:19] sts rem. Fasten off.

Left front

Using size I (6.00mm) hook and A, make 29[31:33:35] ch and work base row as for back. 27[29:31:33] sts. Work 6[8:10:10] rows. Dec 1dc at center of next row. Work 7[9:11:11] rows without

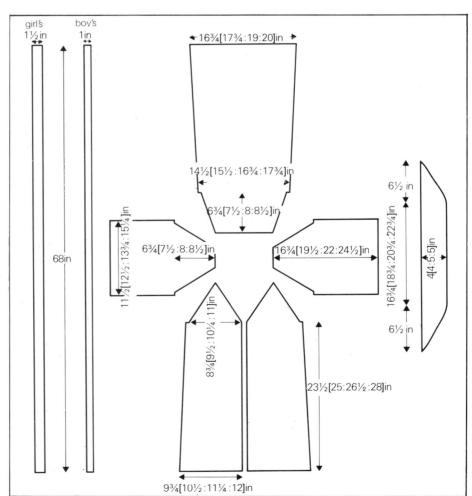

shaping. Rep last 8[10:12:12] rows once more, then work the dec row again: 24[26:28:30]dc. Cont without shaping until work is same length as back up to beg of raglan shaping.

Shape raglan armhole and front edge
1st row Sl st across first 3 sts, 3ch, 1dc into each dc to within last 3 sts, dec 1dc, 1dc into top of turning ch. Turn.
2nd row 3ch, skip first dc, dec 1dc, 1dc into each dc to within last 3 sts, dec 1dc, 1dc into top of turning ch. Turn. Rep last row until one st rem. Fasten off.

Right front

Work as for left front up to beg of raglan shaping.
Shape raglan armhole and front edge
1st row 3ch, skip first dc, dec 1dc, 1dc into each dc to within last 2 sts, turn.
2nd row 3ch, skip first dc, dec 1dc, 1dc into each dc to within last 3 sts, dec 1dc, 1dc into top of turning ch. Turn. Rep last row until one st rem. Fasten off.

Sleeves

Using size I (6.00mm) hook and A, chain 34[36:40:44] and work base row as for back. Cont in dc until sleeve measures 10[12:14:16]in (25[30:35:40]cm) from beg.
Shape raglan armhole
Work as for back raglan armhole shaping until 8[8:10:12] sts rem. Fasten off.

Edging

Join raglan and side seams.
Using size H (5.00mm) hook and with RS facing join A to lower edge at center back and work 1sc into each foundation ch along this edge to corner of right front, work 3sc into first row end, then 2sc into each row end along front edge to top of first sleeve, 1sc into each st along top of sleeve, back neck and second sleeve, then 2sc into each row end along left front edge to within last row end, 3sc into last row end, then 1sc into each foundation ch along lower edge of back, sl st into first sc. Fasten off.

Collar

Using size H (5.00mm) hook and B, make 2ch.
Base row 1sc into 2nd ch from hook. Turn.
1st row 1ch, 1sc into sc. Turn.
2nd row 1ch, 2sc into sc. Turn.
3rd row 1ch, 1sc into each of the 2sc. Turn.
4th row 1ch, 2sc into first sc, 1sc into next sc. Turn.
5th row 1ch, 1sc into each sc. Turn.
6th row 1ch, 2sc into first sc, 1sc into each sc to end. Turn.
7th row 1ch, 1sc into each sc to end. Turn.
Rep last 2 rows until there are 10[10:14:14] sts.
Next row 1ch, 1sc into each sc to end.

Turn.
Rep last row 51[57:64:69] times more.
Next row 1ch, leaving loop of each on hook work 1sc into each of next 2sc, yo and draw a loop through all loops on hook (1sc decreased), 1sc into each sc to end. Turn.
Next row 1ch, 1sc into each sc to end. Turn.
Rep last 2 rows until one st rem. Work 1 row. Fasten off.

Edging

Using size H (5.00mm) hook and with RS facing join B to first sc on right lower front edge, work 1sc into each sc along front edge to collar, 1sc into each row end all around collar, then 1sc into each sc along left front edge, do not turn. Change to size F (4.00mm) hook and work a row of crab st (sc worked from left to right) along left front, around collar and along right front. Fasten off.

Cuffs (alike)

Using size H (5.00mm) hook and B and with RS facing, work 1sc into each foundation ch along lower edge of sleeve. Now work 8[10:12:12] rows in sc; do not turn on last row but work a row of crab st.
Fasten off.
Join seam and turn back cuff.

Pocket

Using size H (5.00mm) hook and B, make 17[17:19:19]ch.
Base row 1sc into 2nd ch from hook, 1sc into each ch to end. Turn.
Next row 1ch, skip first sc, 1sc into each sc to end, 1sc into turning ch. Turn.
Rep last row 14[14:20:20] times more, do not turn on last row but work a row of crab st.
Fasten off.
Sew pocket to left or right front.

Belt

Using size I (6.00mm) hook and 2 strands of B tog throughout, make 3ch, work 1hdc into 3rd ch from hook. Turn.
Next row 2ch, 1hdc into hdc. Turn. Rep last row until belt measures 68in (172cm) or required length.
Fasten off.
For alternative belt, knit as foll: using No. 6 (4½mm) needles and B, cast on 10 sts and work in K1, P1 ribbing until belt measures 68in (172cm) or required length. Bind off in ribbing.

To finish

Make a belt loop on each side seam at waist level and thread belt through. Press lightly with a warm iron over a damp cloth.

Technique tip
Crab stitch edging

Crab stitch is a single crochet edging that is worked in reverse—that is, from left to right instead of right to left, to produce the effects of a textured, bound edge.
Begin by working a row of single crochet along the side of the fabric to be edged. Do not cut off yarn.

Take yarn around hook and draw a loop through, so having 2 loops on hook. Take yarn around hook again and draw it through both loops on hook.

Work in this way into each single crochet.

Make one chain, then insert the hook into the previous single crochet to the right.

Crochet

Baby's overalls and jacket

This colorful outfit will keep any baby happy and snug. The overalls are striped all over, and the jacket is worked with graduated stripes.

Kim Sayer

Sizes
Overalls Crotch to waist, 8¼in (21cm).
Inside leg, 9in (23cm).
Jacket To fit 20in (51cm) chest.
Length, 11in (28cm).
Sleeve length, 6in (15cm) with cuff turned back.

Materials
Overalls *4oz (100g) of a sport weight yarn in main color A*
2oz (50g) in each of 3 contrasting colors B, C and D.
Jacket *6oz (150g) in main color A and 2oz (50g) in contrasting color C*

Note *If you are making the set you will need 9oz (250g) in main color A and 2oz (50g) in each of 3 contrasting colors B, C and D*

Sizes B and E (2.50 and 3.50mm) hooks
2 buttons and a piece of elastic for back of overalls

Gauge
18sc and 22 rows to 4in (10cm) on size E (3.50mm) hook.

Overalls
Back
Using size E (3.50mm) hook and A, chain 50 for top edge. Cut off A, join on B.
Base row 2ch to count as first sc, 1sc into each ch to end.
Turn.
Next row 2ch, 1sc into each sc to end. Change to C.
Turn.
Shape back
1st row 2ch, 1sc into each sc to within last 6sc. Turn.
2nd row As first row, change to D.
3rd row As first row.
4th row As first row, change to A.
5th row As first row.
6th row As first row, change to B.
Next row 2ch, 1sc into each st in A and into the first 3 sts in D.
Turn.
Next row 2ch, 1sc into each st in B and into the first 3 sts in A, change to C.
Next row 2ch, 1sc into each st.
Turn.
Next row 2ch, 1sc into each st to end.
Turn. 50sc. Change to D.
Next row 2ch. 1sc into each sc.
Turn.
Next row 2ch, 1sc into each sc to end.
Change to A.
Turn.
Cont in sc working in stripes of 2 rows A, 2 rows B, 2 rows C and 2 rows D until 6th stripe in A has been completed.
Shape crotch
Next row Using B work across first 25sc for first leg, make 6ch, turn.
Next row 1sc into 3rd ch from hook, 1sc

into each ch, then 1sc into each sc to end.
Turn. 30sc.
Cont in stripe sequence on these 30sc until 6th stripe in A from beg to crotch has been completed. Work a further 3 rows in A. Fasten off.

Second leg
Using B, make 5ch, then work 1sc into each sc across back. Turn.
Next row 2ch, 1sc into each sc to end, 1sc into each of the 5ch.
Turn. 30sc.
Now work to match first leg.

Front
Using size E (3.50mm) hook and B, make 22ch for top edge of bib.
Base row 1sc into 3rd ch from hook, 1sc into each ch to end. Turn.
Next row 2ch, 1sc into each sc to end. Change to C. Turn.
Cont in stripe sequence as for back until 22 rows have been worked, so ending with 2 rows in D. Change to A and work 1 row. Cut off yarns.
Next row Using A, make 15ch, then work 1sc into each sc to end, make 15ch. Change to B. Turn.
Next row 1sc into 3rd ch from hook, 1sc into each of next 14ch, 1sc into each sc across bib, 1sc into each of last 15ch. Turn. 50 sts.
Work 1 row in B. Cont in stripe sequence until body measures same as back to crotch, then complete as for back.
First strap
With RS facing and using size E (3.50mm) hook, join A to bib at waist edge and work 1sc into each row end to top of bib. Do not turn but make 71ch for strap.

Next row 1sc into 3rd ch from hook, 1sc into each ch, 1sc into each sc. Turn.
1st buttonhole row 2ch, 1sc into each sc to within last 25 sts, (3ch, skip next 3sc, 1sc into each of next 5sc) 3 times, 1sc into top of ch. Turn.
2nd buttonhole row 2ch, (1sc into each of next 5sc, 3sc into next loop) 3 times, now work 1sc into each sc. Turn.
Next row 2ch, 1sc into each sc to end. Fasten off.
Second strap
Make 70ch; then, working from top edge of bib, work 1sc into each row end. Turn.
Next row 2ch, 1sc into each sc, 1sc into each ch to end. Turn.
1st buttonhole row 2ch, (1sc into each of next 5sc, 3ch, skip next 3sc) 3 times, now work 1sc into each sc to end. Turn.
2nd buttonhole row 2ch, 1sc into each sc to within first buttonhole, (3sc into next loop 1sc into each of next 5sc) 3 times, 1sc into top of ch. Turn.
Next row 2ch, 1sc into each sc to end. Fasten off.

Patches (make 2)
Using size E (3.50mm) hook and A, make 12ch.
Base row 1sc into 3rd ch from hook, 1sc into each ch to end. Turn.
Work 9 rows in sc.
Edging
Next row 2ch, work 3sc all into first sc, 1sc into each sc to within last sc, 3sc all into last sc, do not turn but cont along side edge working 1sc into each row end to corner, work 3sc all into first foundation ch, then 1sc into each ch to within last ch. 3sc all into last ch, 1sc into each row end to corner, sl st into top of

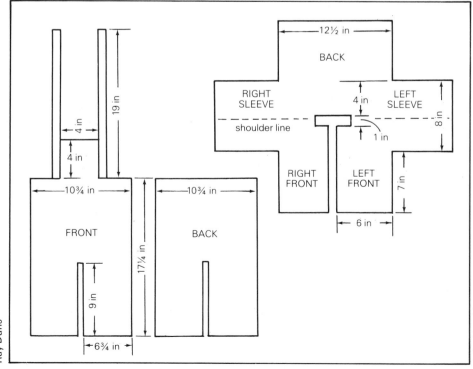

the 2ch. Fasten off.

To finish
Join side and inner leg seams. Work herringbone st casing over elastic on wrong side of back at waist. Sew buttons to top edge of back. Sew on patches.

Jacket (one piece)
Using size E (3.50mm) hook and A, make 58ch for lower edge of back.
Base row 1sc into 3rd ch from hook, 1sc into each ch to end. Turn.
Next row 2ch, 1sc into each sc. Turn. Cont in sc work 2 rows C, 2 rows A, 2 rows C, 4 rows A, 2 rows C, 6 rows A and 2 rows C. Cont with A only, work in sc until work measures 7in (18cm) from beg. Fasten off.
Make 34ch for first sleeve, then work across sts of back, make 35ch for 2nd sleeve. Turn.
Next row 1sc into 3rd ch from hook, 1sc into each ch to end, 1sc into each sc, then 1sc into each ch. 125 sts. Cont in sc until sleeve measures 4in (10cm) in depth, ending at sleeve edge.
Shape neck
Next row Work across first 53 sts, turn. Work 4 rows straight on these 53 sts.
Next row Make 9ch for front neck, 1sc into 3rd ch from hook, 1sc into each of next 6ch, 1sc into each sc to end. Turn. 61 sts.
Cont without shaping until sleeve measures 8in (20cm) in depth, ending at front edge.
Next row Work across first 27 sts. Turn. Work on these 27 sts for right front, until front measures same as back to top of last colored stripe. Now work 2 rows C, 6 rows A, 2 rows C, 4 rows A, (2 rows C, 2 rows A) twice. Fasten off. Skip center 19sc for back neck, rejoin yarn to next sc and work to end. Turn. Work 3 rows straight. Fasten off.
Next row Make 8ch for front neck, then work 1sc into each sc to end. Turn.
Next row Work to end, then work 1sc into each of the 8ch. Turn. 61 sts.
Cont without shaping until sleeve measures 8in (20cm) in depth, ending at side edge. Fasten off. Skip first 34 sts, rejoin yarn and work to end. Now complete to match right front.

Edging
Join side and underarm seams.
With RS facing and using size B (2.50mm) hook, join A to lower edge of right front and work (1sc into each of next 2 row ends, skip next row end) along right front to neck, 1sc into each st across front neck, 1sc into each row end up side neck, 1sc into each st across back neck, 1sc into each row end on other side of neck, 1sc into each st across front neck and (1sc into each of next 2 row ends, skip next row end) to lower edge. Fasten off. Join C to last sc worked and work a

row of crab stitch (sc worked from left to right) all around outer edge of jacket. Fasten off.

Sleeve edgings
With WS facing and using size B (2.50mm) hook join on A and work 1sc into each row end, sl st into first sc. Now work a round of crab stitch. Fasten off.

Turn work to RS, turn back first 6 rows of sleeve; then, using C and working into fold, work a row of crab stitch. Fasten off.

Ties (make 4) Using size E (3.50mm) hook and 2 strands of C tog make a ch approx. 12½in (32cm) long. Fasten off. Sew one tie to each side of neck and other two approx. 3¼in (8cm) below.

79

CROCHET

Sizes
To fit 26[28:30]in (66[71:76]cm) chest.
Length, 16½[18:19½]in (42[46:50])cm).
Sleeve seam, 15[15¾:16½]in
(38[40:42]cm).

Note directions for larger sizes are in
brackets []; where there is only one set
of figures it applies to all sizes.

Materials
*22[23:25]oz (600[650:700]g) of a
knitting worsted in main color (A)
4oz (100g) in a contrasting color (B)
Sizes G and H (4.50 and 5.50mm)
hooks
Open-ended zipper for front
4in (10cm) zipper for pocket
6in (15cm) square of fabric*

Gauge
14 sts and 14 rows to 4in (10cm) in patt
on size H (5.50mm) hook.

Back
** Using size G (4.50mm) hook and B,
make 52[56:60]ch.
Base row 1sc into 3rd ch from hook, 1sc
into each ch to end. Turn.
Next row 2ch to count as first sc, 1sc into
each sc to end. Turn.
Rep last row 4 times more. Cut off B, join
on A. Change to size H (5.50mm) hook.
Work 2 rows in sc. Beg patt.
1st row (RS) 3ch to count as first dc,
*1dc into next dc, work around next dc by
working yo, insert hook from front to back
between next 2dc, around dc at left and
through work from back to front; draw
yarn through and complete dc in usual
way—called double around front (dc
around Ft), rep from * to within last 2sc,
1dc into next sc, 1dc into turning ch. Turn.
2nd row 2ch, 1sc into each st. Turn.
3rd row 3ch, *work 1dc around Ft
working around next dc on first row, skip
sc above this dc, 1dc into next sc, rep from
* to end, working last dc into turning ch.
Turn.
4th row As 2nd row.
5th row 3ch, 1dc into next sc, *1dc
around front working around next dc on
3rd row, skip sc above this dc, 1dc into
next sc, rep from * to within turning ch,
1dc into turning ch. Turn.
2nd to 5th rows form patt. * Cont in patt
until work measures 11[11¾:12½]in (28
[30:32]cm) from beg; end with WS row.
Shape armholes
Next row Sl st over first 5 sts, patt to

One for the boys

This bomber jacket has a thick
textured basket weave pattern
for extra warmth. Contrasting
collar, cuffs and waistband add
a touch of style.

Serge Krouglikoff

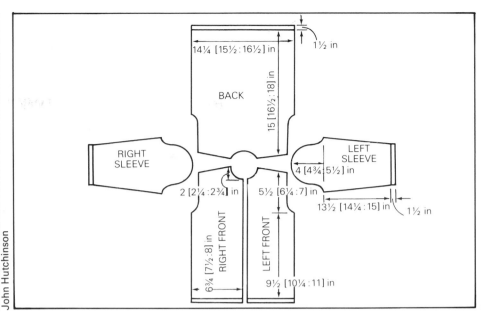

Diagram labels:
- 14¼ [15½ : 16½] in
- 1½ in
- BACK
- 15 [16½ : 18] in
- RIGHT SLEEVE
- LEFT SLEEVE
- 4 [4¾ : 5½] in
- 2 [2¼ : 2¾] in
- 5½ [6¼ : 7] in
- 13½ [14¼ : 15] in
- 1½ in
- 6¾ [7½ : 8] in
- RIGHT FRONT
- LEFT FRONT
- 9½ [10¼ : 11] in

John Hutchinson

within last 4sts, turn.
Dec one st at each end of next 2[3:4] rows by working 2sc tog. 39[41:43] sc. Cont straight until work measures 5½[6¼:7]in (14[16:18]cm) from beg of armhole; end with WS row.

Shape shoulders
Next row Sl st over first 5[5:6] sts, patt over next 5[6:6] sts. Fasten off. Skip next 19 sts, rejoin yarn to next st, patt over the next 5[6:6] sts. Fasten off.

Left front
Using size G (4.50mm) hook and B, make 26[28:30]ch. Work as for back from ** to **. Cont in patt until work measures 5½in (14cm) from beg; end with WS row.
Pocket row Patt over first 5[6:7] sts, make 15ch, skip next 15 sts, patt over last 5[6:7] sts. Turn. Cont in patt, working into ch on next row, until front measures same as back to armhole; end with WS row.

Shape armhole
Next row Sl st over first 5 sts, patt to end. Turn. 19[20:21] sts. Dec one st at armhole edge on next 2[3:4] rows. Cont straight until work measures 3½[4:4¼]in (9[10:11]cm) from beg of armhole; end with WS row.

Shape neck
Next row Patt to last 4 sts, turn. Dec one st at neck edge on next 5 rows, then cont straight until armhole measures same as back, up to beg of shoulder; end with WS row.

Shape shoulder
Next row Sl st over first 5[5:6] sts, patt to end. Fasten off.

Right front
Work to match left front, omitting pocket and reversing all shaping.

Sleeves
Using size G (4.50mm) hook and B, make 22[24:26] ch. Work base row as for back, then work 5 rows in sc, inc 4[4:6]sc evenly on last row by working 2sc into a sc. 25[27:31]sc. Cut off B, join on A. Change to size H (5.50mm) hook and work 2 rows sc. Cont in patt as for back but inc one st at each end of 3rd and every foll 8th row until there are 35[39:43] sts. Cont straight until sleeve measures 15[15¾:16½]in (38[40:42]cm) from beg; end with WS row

Shape top
Next row Sl st over first 5 sts, patt to last 4 sts. Turn. Work 1 row. Dec one st at each end of next and foll 3[4:5] alternate rows, then at each end of every row until 9 sts rem. Fasten off.

Collar
Using size G (4.50mm) hook and B, make 57[61:65]ch loosely. Work base row as for back, then work 3 rows in sc.
Next row 2ch, 1sc into each of next 5[4:5]sc, *work next 2sc tog, 1sc into each of next 12[10:8]sc, rep from * 2[3:4] times more, work next 2sc tog, 1sc into each sc to end. Turn. 52[55:58]sc. Work 3 rows.
Next row 2ch, 1sc into each of next 5[4:5]sc, *work next 2sc tog, 1sc into each of next 11[9:7]sc, rep from * 2[3:4] times more, work next 2sc, 1sc into each sc to end. Turn. 48[50:52]sc. Work 1[3:5] rows.
Next row Sl st over first 5 sts, patt to within last 4 sts. Turn.
Rep last row 3 times more. Fasten off.

To finish
Join shoulder seams. Set in sleeves, join side and sleeve seams. Sew in pocket zipper. Trim pocket fabric to size, hem and sew in place. Using size G (4.50mm) hook, work 2 rows of sc along each front edge, matching colors. Sew on collar and zipper. Press seams.

Guernsey fisherman's sweaters

We have adapted a traditional Guernsey fisherman's pattern to make these two nautical sweaters. For the yoke choose either the tree of life pattern or the flag and ladder pattern.

Sizes
To fit 32[34:36:38:40:42]in (83[87:92:97:102:107]cm) bust/chest.
Length, 23½[24½:25:26:27:27½]in (60[62:64:66:68:70]cm).
Sleeve seam, 17[17¼:17¾:18:18½:19]in (43[44:45:46:47:48]cm).
Note Directions for larger sizes are in brackets []; where there is only one set of figures it applies to all sizes.

Materials
- 23[25:29:30:34:36]oz (650[700:800:850:950:1000]g) of a knitting worsted
- 1 pair each Nos. 4 and 6 (3¾ and 4½mm) knitting needles
- 1 cable needle

Gauge
20 sts and 28 rows to 4in (10cm) in stockinette st on No. 6 (4½mm) needles.

Note In this pattern the abbreviation C4 is used; this means cable 4, which is worked as follows: place next 2 sts onto cable needle and leave at back of work, K2, then K the sts from cable needle.

Back and front (alike)
Using No. 4 (3¾mm) needles cast on 85 [91:97:103:109:115] sts.
1st ribbing row K1, (P1, K1) to end.
2nd ribbing row P1, (K1, P1) to end.
Rep these 2 rows for 3½in (8cm), ending with a 2nd row. Change to No. 6 (4½mm) needles. Beg with a K row, cont in stockinette st until work measures 15½[15¾:16¼:16½:17:17½]in (39[40:41:42:43:44]cm) from beg, ending with a P row.
Change to No. 4 (3¾mm) needles and K5 rows, so ending with a RS row.
Change to No. 6 (4½mm) needles.

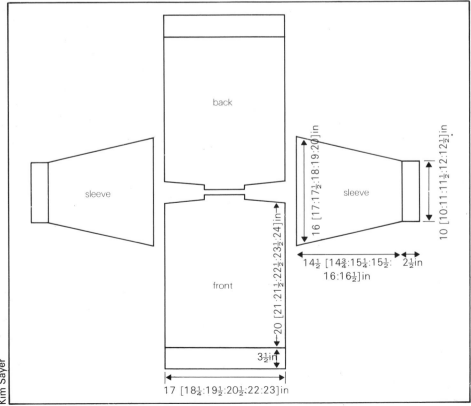

back

sleeve

sleeve

16 [17:17½:18:19:20]in

10 [10:11:11½:12:12½]in

14½ [14¾:15¼:15½: 16:16½]in   2½in

20 [21:21½:22½:23½:24]in

front

3½in

17 [18¼:19½:20½:22:23]in

For tree of life patterned yoke:

Next row K to end, but for 1st, 2nd and 3rd sizes only dec one st at center of row and for 4th, 5th and 6th sizes only inc one st each end of row. 84 [90:96:105:111:117] sts. Commence patt.

1st row For 1st and 4th sizes only P4, for 2nd and 5th sizes only P1, K4, P2, for 3rd and 6th sizes only P4, K4, P2, then for all sizes * K6, P1, K6, P2, K4, P2*, rep from * to * 2[2:2:3:3:3] times more, K6, P1, K6, then for 1st and 4th sizes only P4 for 2nd and 5th sizes only P2, K4, P1, for 3rd and 6th sizes only P2, K4, P4.

2nd row For 1st and 4th sizes only K4, for 2nd and 5th sizes only K1, P4, K2, for 3rd and 6th sizes only K4, P4, K2 then for all sizes *P5, K1, P1, K1, P5, K2, P4, K2*, rep from * to * 2[2:2:3:3:3] times more, P5, K1, P1, K1, P5, then for 1st and 4th sizes only K4, for 2nd and 5th sizes only K2, P4, K1, for 3rd and 6th sizes only K2, P4, K4.

3rd row For 1st and 4th sizes only P4, for 2nd and 5th sizes only P1, C4, P2, for 3rd and 6th sizes only P4, C4, P2, then for all sizes *K4, P1, K3, P1, K4, P2, C4, P2*, rep from * to * 2[2:2:3:3:3] times more, K4, P1, K3, P1, K4, then for 1st and 4th sizes only P4, for 2nd and 5th sizes only P2, C4, P1, for 3rd and 6th sizes only P2, C4, P4.

4th row Patt 4[7:10:4:7:10] sts as 2nd row, *P3, K1, (P2, K1) twice, P3, K2, P4, K2*, rep from * to * 2[2:2:3:3:3] times more, P3, K1, (P2, K1) twice, P3, patt to end as 2nd row.

5th row Patt 4[7:10:4:7:10] sts as first row, *(K2, P1) twice, K1, (P1, K2) twice, P2, K4, P2*, rep from * to * 2[2:2:3:3:3] times more, (K2, P1) twice, K1, (P1, K2) twice, patt to end as first row.

6th row Patt 4[7:10:4:7:10] sts as 2nd row, *P1, K1, P2, K1, P3, K1, P3, K1, P2, K1, P1, K2, P4, K2*, rep from * to * 2[2:2:3:3:3] times more, P1, K1, P2, K1, P3, K1, P2, K1, P1, patt to end as 2nd row.

7th row Patt 4[7:10:4:7:10] sts as first row, *K3, (P1, K2) twice, P1, K3, P2, K4, P2*, rep from * to * 2[2:2:3:3:3] times more, K3, P1, (K2, P1) twice, K3, patt to end.

8th row Patt 4[7:10:4:7:10] sts as 2nd row, *(P2, K1) twice, P1, (K1, P2) twice, K2, P4, K2*, rep from * to * 2[2:2:3:3:3] times more, (P2, K1) twice, P1, (K1, P2) twice, patt to end.

9th row As 3rd row.

10th row As 4th row.

11th row Pat 4[7:10:4:7:10] sts as first row, *K5, P1, K1, P1, K5, P2, K4, P2, rep from * to * 2[2:2:3:3:3] times more, K5, P1, K1, P1, K5, patt to end.

12th row Patt 4[7:10:4:7:10] sts as 2nd row, *P4, K1, P3, K1, P4, K2, P4, K2*, rep from * to * 2[2:2:3:3:3] times

more, P4, K1, P3, K1, P4, patt to end.

13th row As first row.

14th row Patt 4[7:10:4:7:10] sts as 2nd row, *P5, K3, P5, K2, P4, K2*, rep from * to * 2[2:2:3:3:3] times more, P5, K3, P5, patt to end.

15th row Patt 4[7:10:4:7:10] sts as 3rd row *K6, P1, K6, P2, C4, P2*, rep from * to * 2[2:2:3:3:3] times more, K6, P1, K6, patt to end as 3rd row.

16th row Patt 4[7:10:4:7:10] sts as 2nd row, *P13, K2, P4, K2*, rep from * to * 2[2:2:3:3:3] times more, P13, patt to end.

17th row Patt 4[7:10:4:7:10] sts as first row, *K13, P2, K4, P2*, rep from * to * 2[2:2:3:3:3] times, K13, patt to end.

18th row As 16th row.

These 18 rows form the patt. Cont in patt until work measures 23½[24½:25:26:27:27½] in (60[62:64:66:68:70]cm) from beg, ending with a WS row.

Shape shoulders
Keeping patt correct, bind off 6[7:7:8:9:9] sts at beg of next 6 rows and 7[6:8:8:7:9] sts at beg of foll 2 rows. 34[36:38:41:43:45] sts rem. Change to No. 4 (3¾mm) needles and cont in ribbing as at beg, inc one st in center of first row on 1st, 2nd and 3rd sizes, rib 6 rows. Bind off in ribbing.

For flag and ladder patt yoke:
Next row K to end, but for 1st and 4th sizes only inc one st at each end of row. 87[91:97:105:109:115] sts. Commence patt.
1st row P0[0:1:0:0:1], (K1, P1) 1[2:3:1:2:3] times, *K1, P9, (K1, P1) 4 times*, rep from * to * 3[3:3:4:4:4] times more, K1, P9, K1, (P1, K1) 1[2:3:1:2:3] times, P0[0:1:0:0:1].
2nd row K0[0:3:0:0:3], P0[1:1:0:1:1], K2[3:3:2:3:3], *P1, K8, P2, K3, P1, K3*, rep from * to 3[3:3:4:4:4] times more, P1, K8, P2, K2[3:3:2:3:3], P0[1:1:0:1:1], K0[0:3:0:0:3].
3rd row Patt 2[4:7:2:4:7] sts as first row, *K3, P7, (K1, P1) 4 times*, rep from * to * 3[3:3:4:4:4] times more, K3, P7, K1, patt to end as first row.
4th row Patt 2[4:7:2:4:7] sts as 2nd row, *P1, K6, P4, K3, P1, K3*, rep from * to * 3[3:3:4:4:4] times more, P1, K6, P4, patt to end as 2nd row.
5th row Patt 2[4:7:2:4:7] sts as first row, *K5, P5, (K1, P1) 4 times*, rep from * to * 3[3:3:4:4:4] times more, K5, P5, K1, patt to end as first row.
6th row Patt 2[4:7:2:4:7] sts as 2nd row, *P1, K4, P6, K3, P1, K3*, rep from * to * 3[3:3:4:4:4] times more, P1, K4, P6, patt to end as 2nd row.
7th row Patt 2[4:7:2:4:7] sts as first row, *K7, P3, (K1, P1) 4 times*, rep from * to * 3[3:3:4:4:4] times more, K7, P3, K1, patt to end as first row.
8th row Patt 2[4:7:2:4:7] sts as 2nd row, *P1, K2, P8, K3, P1, K3*, rep from * to * 3[3:3:4:4:4] times more, P1, K2, P8, patt to end as 2nd row.
9th row Patt 2[4:7:2:4:7] sts as first row, *K9, P1, (K1, P1) 4 times*, rep from * to * 3[3:3:4:4:4] times more, K9, P1, K1, patt to end as first row.
10th row Patt 2[4:7:2:4:7] sts as 2nd row, *P11, K3, P1, K3*, rep from * to * 3[3:3:4:4:4] times more, P11, patt to end as 2nd row.
These 10 rows form the patt. Cont in patt until work measures 23½[24½:25:26:27:27½]in (60[62:64:66:68:70]cm) from beg, ending with a WS row.
Shape shoulders
Keeping patt correct, bind off 6[7:7:8:9:9] sts at beg of next 6 rows and 7[6:8:8:7:9] sts at beg of foll 2 rows. 34[36:38:41:43:45] sts rem. Change to No. 4 (3¾mm) needles and work 6 rows in ribbing. Bind off loosely in ribbing.

Sleeves

Using No. 4 (3¾mm) needles cast on 43[45:47:49:51:53] sts and work in ribbing as for back and front for 2½in (6cm), ending with a 2nd row and inc 6[6:8:8:10:10] sts evenly across last row. 49[51:55:57:61:63] sts.

Change to No. 6 (4½mm) needles. Beg with a K row, cont in stockinette st, inc one st at each end of 5th and every foll 6th row until there are 79 [83:87:91:95:99] sts, then cont without shaping until work measures 16¼[16½:17:17¼:17¾:18¼]in

(41[42:43:44:45:46]cm); end with P row. K6 rows, then bind off very loosely.

To finish

Press work with a warm iron over a damp cloth. Join shoulder and neckband seams. Sew sleeves to body. Join side and sleeve seams.

Technique tip

Setting in the sleeves

A feature of a traditional "Guernsey" is the dropped shoulder line, which we have incorporated in our Guernsey-style sweaters. The body is worked straight to the shoulder shaping, rather than being decreased at the armholes, forming the dropped shoulder line when it is worn.

Because no armhole shaping is worked on the body there is no need to work a sleeve head. The sleeves are knitted until they are the desired width and length and then the knitting is bound off very loosely. If the knitting is bound off too tightly the sleeve will restrict the armhole depth.

To set in a sleeve of this kind, first join the shoulder seams (a).

Mark the center of the bound off edge of the sleeve with a pin (b).

Placing the two pieces of knitting with right sides together, match the pin to the shoulder seam, then pin the sleeve to the back and front sections (c). Sew the sleeve in position. You will see that the armhole depth has now been established. Set in the other sleeve in the same way to complete the sweater (d).

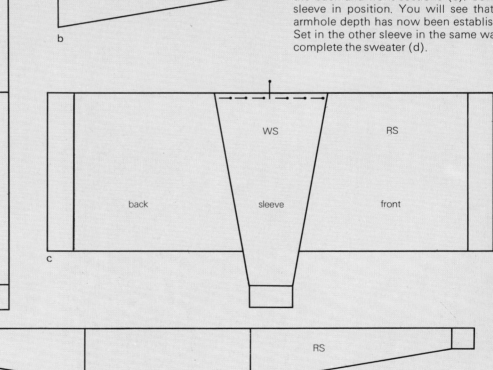

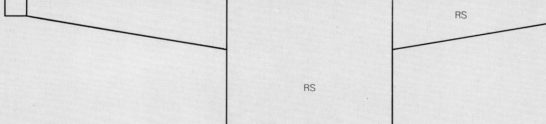

Cotton on

These attractive motifs are just the thing to add a dash of color to a simple sweater. It's easy to knit them in, following the charts on the next two pages.

Steve Bicknell

Size

To fit 24[26:28]in (61[66:71]cm) chest.
Length, 15¾[17¼:19]in (40[44:48]cm).
Sleeve, 12¾[14¼:15¾]in (32[36:40]cm).
Note Directions for larger sizes are in brackets []; where there is only one set of figures it applies to all sizes.

Materials (for each sweater)

9[11:11]oz (250[300:300]g) med.-weight cotton yarn in main color (A)
6oz (150g) of a med.-weight cotton yarn in contrasting color (B)
1 pair each Nos. 4 and 6 (3¾ and 4½mm) needles

Gauge

Kite sweater: 18 sts and 32 rows to 4in (10cm) in garter st using No. 6 (4½mm) needles.
Train sweater: 18 sts and 30 rows to 4in (10cm) in seed st using No. 6 (4½mm) needles.

Kite sweater

Back
** Using No. 4 (3¾mm) needles and B, cast on 61[65:69] sts.
1st ribbing row (K1, P1) to last st, K1.
2nd ribbing row (P1, K1) to last st, P1.
Rep these 2 rows 6 times more. Cut off B and join on A. Change to No. 6 (4½mm) needles **. Using A, cont in garter st until work measures 13¾[15¼:17]in (35[39:43]cm) from beg; end with WS row.
Inc row K1[5:9] sts, *inc in next st, K5, rep from * to end. 71[75:79] sts. Cut off A and join on B. Change to No. 4 (3¾mm) needles. P1 row. Rep 2 ribbing rows 6 times, then work first ribbing row again. Bind off loosely in ribbing.

Front
Work as for back from ** to **.
Cont in garter st until work measures 2¼[3:3½]in (6[8:9]cm) from beg; end with WS row. Beg motif, twisting yarn when changing color to avoid making a hole.
1st row K30[32:34] sts in A, 8 sts in B, 23[25:27] sts in A.
2nd row K23[25:27] sts in A, 8 sts in B, 30[32:34] sts in A.
Reading RS rows from right to left and WS rows from left to right, beg row 3 of chart, cont in garter until 68th row has been completed. Cut off B. With A only, cont in garter st until work measures 13¾[15¼:17]in (35[39:43]cm) from beg; end with WS row.
Inc row K1[5:9] sts, *inc in next st, K5, rep from * to end. 71[75:79] sts. Cut off A and join on B. Change to No. 4 (3¾mm) needles. P1 row, then rib 13 rows as for back.
Bind off loosely in ribbing.

Sleeves
Using No. 4 (3¾mm) needles and B, cast on 33[35:37] sts. Rib 18 rows as for back. Cut off B and join on A. Change to No. 6 (4½mm) needles and cont in garter st, inc one st at each end of every foll 6th row until there are 53[57:61] sts.

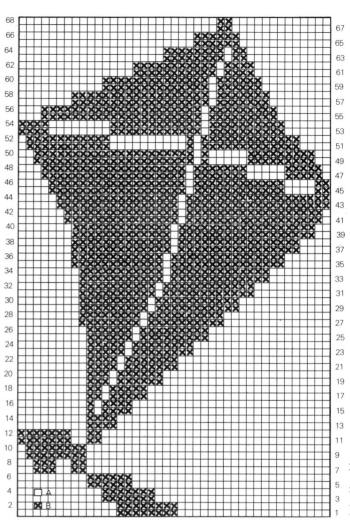

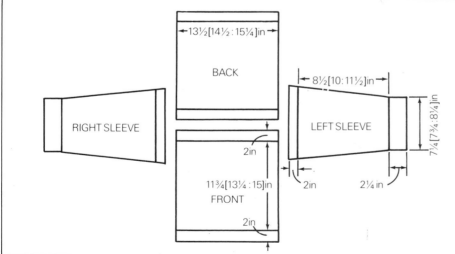

Cont without shaping until work measures 10¾[12¼:13¾]in (27[31:35]cm) from beg; end with WS row.

Inc row K4[3:7] sts, *inc in next st, K5, rep from * to end. 62[66:70] sts. Cut off A and join on B. Change to No. 4 (3¾mm) needles. P1 row, then rib 13 rows as for back. Bind off loosely in ribbing.

To finish
Press lightly, omitting ribbing. Join back and front tog at shoulders for 3¼[3½: 3½]in (8[9:9]cm), so leaving center open for neck. Mark center of bound-off edge of sleeves with a pin, match pin to shoulder seams. Sew sleeves to body. Join rem seams. Press lightly. Follow washing/cleaning directions on yarn wrappers.

Train sweater

Back
** Using No. 4 (3¾mm) needles and B, cast on 61[65:69] sts.
1st ribbing row (K1, P1) to last st, K1.
2nd ribbing row (P1, K1) to last st, P1.
Rep these 2 rows 6 times more. Cut off B and join on A. Change to No. 6 (4½mm) needles. **
K1 row.
Next row K1, * P1, K1, rep from * to end. This row forms seed st patt. Cont in seed st until work measures 13¾[15¼:17]in (35[39:43]cm) from beg; end with RS row.
Inc row Seed st 1[5:9] sts, * inc in next st, seed 5, rep from * to end. 71[75:79] sts. Cut off A and join on B. Change to No. 4 (3¾mm) needles. K1 row. Rep 2 ribbing rows 6 times, then work 2nd ribbing row again.
Bind off loosely in ribbing.

Front
Work as given for back from ** to **. Cont in seed st until work measures 2¼[3:3½]in (6[8:9]cm) from beg; end with WS row.
Beg motif, twisting yarn when changing

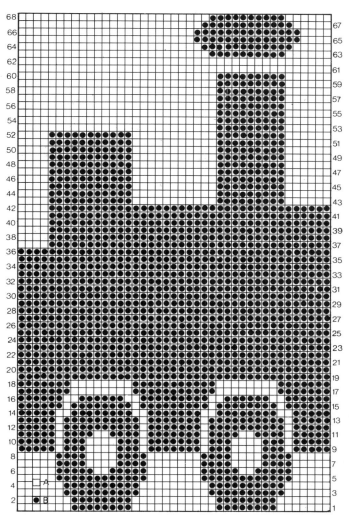

John Hutchinson

color to avoid a hole.

1st row Seed st 17[19:21] sts in A, 8 sts in B, 11 sts in A, 8 sts in B and 17[19:21] sts in A.

2nd row Seed st 17[19:21] sts in A, 8 sts in B, 11 sts in A, 8 sts in B and 17[19:21] sts in A.

Reading RS rows from right to left and WS rows from left to right, beg row 3 of chart, cont in seed st until 68th row has been completed. Cut off B. With A only, cont in seed st until work measures 13¾[15¼:17]in (35[39:43]cm) from beg; end with RS row. Complete front as for back.

Sleeves

Using No. 4 (3¾mm) needles and B cast on 33[35:37] sts. Rib 18 rows as for back. Cut off B and join on A. Change to No. 6 (4½mm) needles.

K1 row.

Cont in seed st, inc one st at each end of every foll 6th row until there are 53[57: 61] sts. Cont without shaping until work measures 10¾[12¼:13¾]in (27[31:35]cm) from beg; end with RS row.

Next row Seed st 0[3:0] sts, *inc in next st, K5, rep from * to end. 62[66:70] sts.

Cut off A and join on B. Change to No. 4 (3¾mm) needles, K1 row, then rib 13 rows as for back.

Bind off loosely in ribbing.

To finish

Complete as given in directions for Kite sweater. Follow washing/cleaning directions on yarn wrappers.

Technique tip

Working ribbing at the top of a section

If you want to work a ribbed section at the top of a garment, using a smaller needle size, you will need to increase across the top of the main section —otherwise, the ribbed section will be too narrow.

Some patterns provide detailed directions for the increase row; others simply tell you to increase a certain number of stitches evenly across the row. In either case, work the increase row in the main fabric yarn.

On changing to the new color work one row in either knit or purl—depending upon whether this is a right-, or wrong-side row—before beginning. In this way you keep the broken line—caused by changing color—on the wrong side.

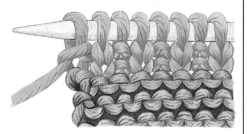

Above, the wrong side of work with a few rows of ribbing completed. Below, the right side.

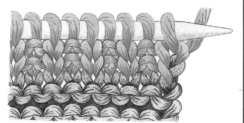

Coral Mula

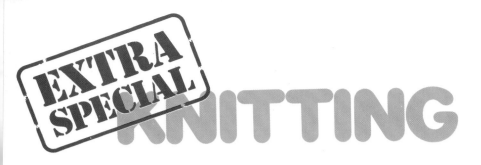

EXTRA SPECIAL KNITTING

Raspberries and cream

Here's a fashion to feast your eyes on—a delectable creamy sweater knitted in a lacy pattern and trimmed with a fluted collar teamed with a svelte cardigan with an open V neck.

Sizes
To fit 34[36:38]in (87[92:97]cm) bust.
Sweater length, $20\frac{3}{4}$[21:$21\frac{1}{2}$]in (53[54:55]cm).
Sleeve seam, $17\frac{1}{2}$in (44cm).
Cardigan length, 24[24:$24\frac{1}{2}$]in (61[61:62]cm).
Sleeve seam, $17\frac{1}{4}$in (44cm).

Note Directions for larger sizes are in brackets[]; where there is only one set of figures it applies to all sizes.

Materials
Sweater 13[13:15]oz (350[350:400]g) of a knitting worsted
1 pair each Nos. 3 and 5 ($3\frac{1}{4}$mm and 4mm) knitting needles
Cardigan 16[18:18]oz (450[500:500]g) of a bulky-weight yarn
1 pair each Nos. 7 and 9 (5mm and 6mm) knitting needles
4 buttons

Gauge
Sweater: 22 sts and 30 rows to 4in (10cm) over stockinette stitch worked on No. 5 (4mm) needles.
Cardigan: 15 sts and 20 rows to 4in (10cm) over stockinette stitch worked on No. 9 (6mm) needles.

Sweater

Back
** Using No. 3 ($3\frac{1}{4}$mm) needles cast on 90[96:102] sts.
1st row P2[1:2], K2, *P2, K2, rep from * to last 2[1:2] sts, P2[1:2].
2nd row K2[1:2], P2, *K2, P2, rep from * to last 2[1:2] sts, K2[1:2].
Rep these 2 rows for $3\frac{1}{2}$in (9cm), ending with a 1st row. Change to No. 5 (4mm) needles.
Next row (inc row) P4[7:5], P into front and back of next st—called inc 1—*P7[7:8], inc 1, rep from * to last 5[8:6] sts, P to the end of the row.
101[107:113] sts.
Commence patt.
1st row K to end.
2nd and foll alternate rows P to end.
3rd row K6[5:4], *yo, sl1, K1, psso, K6, rep from * ending K5[4:3] instead of K6.
5th row K4[3:2], K2 tog, yo, K1, yo, sl1, K1, psso, *K3, K2 tog, yo, K1, yo, sl1, K1, psso, rep from * to last 4[3:2] sts, K to end.
7th row As 3rd
9th row K to end.
11th row K10[9:8], *yo, sl1, K1, psso, K6, rep from * ending K9[8:7] instead of K6.
13th row K8[7:6], *K2 tog, yo, K1, yo, sl1, K1, psso, K3, rep from * to last 5[4:3] sts, K to end.
15th row As 11th
16th row P to end.
These 16 rows form the patt. Cont in patt until work measures $12\frac{1}{4}$[$12\frac{1}{2}$:$12\frac{1}{2}$]in (31[32:32]cm) from beg, ending with a P row.
Mark each end of lst row to indicate start of shaping for armhole.

Shape raglan armholes
1st row K2, sl1, K1, psso, patt to last 4 sts, K2 tog, K2.
2nd row P2, P2 tog, P to last 4 sts, P2 tog tbl, P2.
Rep last 2 rows 3[4:5] times more.
Next row As first.
Next row P to end. **
Rep last 2 rows until 27 sts remain, ending with a P row. Bind off.

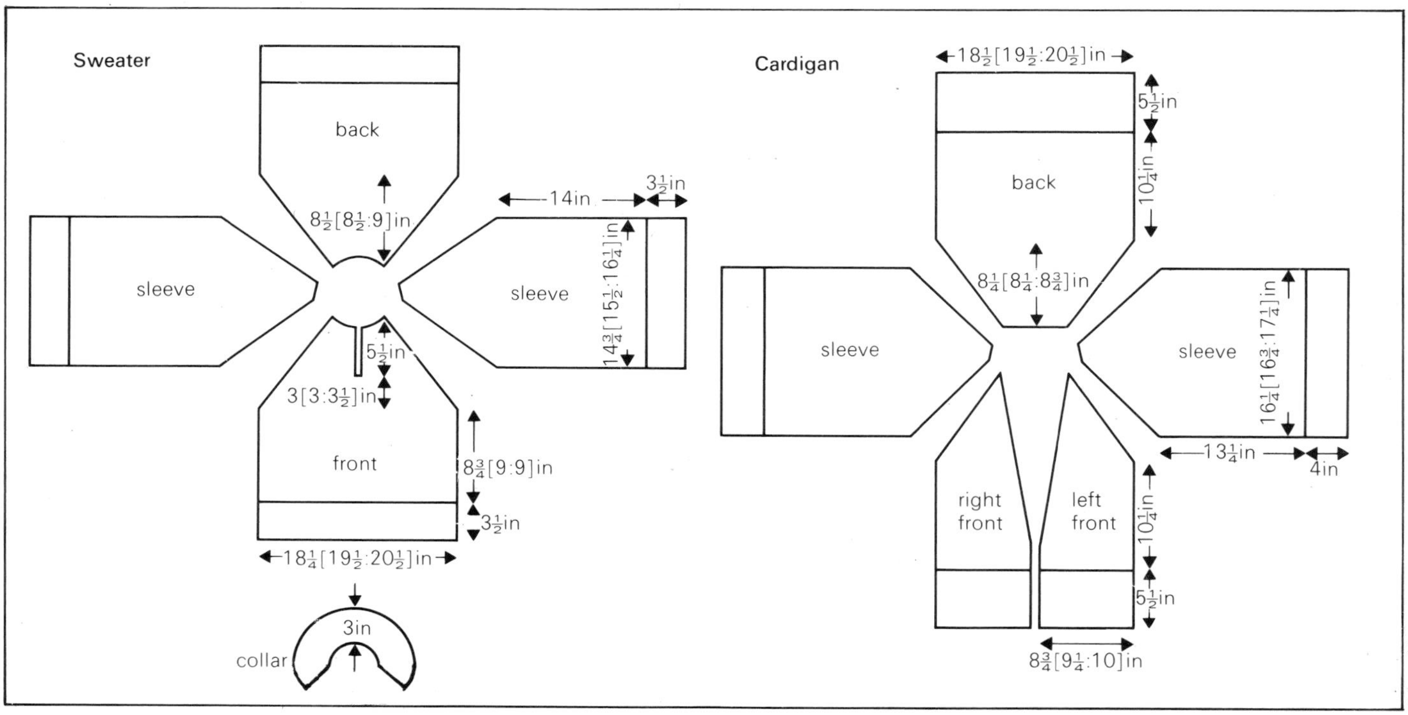
Sweater
back
$8\frac{1}{2}$[$8\frac{1}{2}$:9]in
sleeve
sleeve
14in
$3\frac{1}{2}$in
$14\frac{3}{4}$[$15\frac{1}{2}$:$16\frac{1}{4}$]in
$5\frac{1}{2}$in
3[3:$3\frac{1}{2}$]in
front
$8\frac{3}{4}$[9:9]in
$3\frac{1}{2}$in
$18\frac{1}{4}$[$19\frac{1}{2}$:$20\frac{1}{2}$]in
3in
collar
Cardigan
$18\frac{1}{2}$[$19\frac{1}{2}$:$20\frac{1}{2}$]in
$5\frac{1}{2}$in
back
$10\frac{1}{4}$in
$8\frac{1}{4}$[$8\frac{1}{4}$:$8\frac{3}{4}$]in
sleeve
sleeve
$16\frac{1}{4}$[$16\frac{3}{4}$:$17\frac{1}{4}$]in
$13\frac{1}{4}$in
4in
right front
left front
$10\frac{1}{4}$in
$5\frac{1}{2}$in
$8\frac{3}{4}$[$9\frac{1}{4}$:10]in

Brian Mavor

Front

Work as given for back from ** to **
Rep last 2 rows 4[5:6] times more, then
first row again. 73 sts.
Next row P36, inc 1, P to end.

Shape reglan armhole and divide for front opening

Next row K2, sl1, K1, psso, patt 33 sts,
turn and leave rem sts on a spare needle.
Complete left side of opening first.
Cont on these sts, keeping one st at
opening edge in garter st, and dec for
raglan armhole on every other row until 21
sts rem, ending at opening edge.
Shape neck

Next row Bind off 7 sts, P to end.
Cont to dec for raglan armhole on next
and every other row, *at the same
time* dec one st at neck edge on next
4 rows and then every other row 3
times. K rem 2 sts tog. Fasten off.
With RS of work facing, rejoin yarn to
rem sts for right side of opening, patt
to last 4 sts, K2 tog, K2. Complete to
match other side reversing shapings.

Left sleeve

*** Using No. 3 (3¼mm) needles cast on
48[50:52] sts.
1st row P1[2:1], K2, *P2, K2, rep from
* to last 1[2:1] sts, P1[2:1].

2nd row K1[2:1], P2, *K2, P2, rep from
* to last 1[2:1] sts, K1[2:1].
Rep these 2 rows for 3½in (9cm). End
with a first row. Change to No. 5 (4mm)
needles.
1st size only
Next row P3, P into front and back of
each of next 3 sts, *P1, P into front and
back of each of next 3 sts, rep from * to last
2 sts, P2. 81 sts.
2nd size only
Next row P2, *P into front and back of
each of next 3 sts, P1, rep from * to last
4 sts, P into front and back of each of next
2 sts, P2. 85 sts.
3rd size only

Serge Krouglikoff

Next row P2, *P into front and back of each of next 3 sts, P1, rep from * to last 2 sts, P into front and back of next st, P1. 89 sts.

All sizes
Commence patt.
1st row K to end.
2nd row P to end.
3rd row K4[6:4], * yo, sl1, K1, psso, K6, rep from * ending K3[5:3] instead of K6.
Cont in patt as set until sleeve measures 17½in (44cm) from beg, ending with a P row. Mark each end of last row to denote start of sleeve top.
Shape raglan armhole
1st row K2, sl1, K1, psso, patt to last 4 sts, K2 tog, K2.
2nd row P2, P2 tog, P to last 4 sts, P2 tog tbl, P2.
Rep these 2 rows 3 times more.
Next row As first row.
Next row P to end.
Rep last 2 rows until 11 sts remain, ending with a P row. ***
Shape for neck
1st row K2, sl1, K1, psso, K3, bind off rem 4 sts. Cut off yarn.
Turn and rejoin yarn to rem sts.
2nd row P2 tog, P to end.
3rd row K1, sl1, K1, psso, K2 tog.
4th row P2 tog, P1.
K2 tog and fasten off.

Right sleeve
Work as given for left sleeve from ***
to ***.
Shape for neck
Next row Bind off 4 sts, K until there are 3 sts on right-hand needle, K2 tog, K2. Complete to match left sleeve.

Collar
Using No. 5 (4mm) needles cast on 14 sts.
Next row P to end.
Commence patt.
1st row (RS) K1, P10, inc in next st, K2.
2nd row K to end.
3rd row K1, P11, inc in next st, K2.
4th row K14, turn, P11, inc in next st, K2.
5th row K to end.
6th row K1, P1, (yo, P2 tog) 6 times, P1, K2.
7th row K15, turn, P11, P2 tog, K2.
8th row K to end.
9th row K1, P11, P2 tog, K2.
10th row K to end.
11th row K1, P10, P2 tog, K2.
12th row K to end.
13th row K to end.
14th row K2, P10, turn, K12.
15th row As 14th row.
16th row K2, P11, K1.
Rep these 16 rows 8 times more, then 1st to 13th rows again. Bind off knitwise. Now with RS of work facing pick up and K one st for each 2 rows along the shorter side edge (61 sts).

Beg with a P row, work 7 rows stockinette st. Bind off.

To finish
Do not press. Join raglan seams. Join side and sleeve seams. Sew loosely bound-off edge of collar to neck edge.
Ties (make 2)
Using four 30in (76cm) lengths of yarn together make a twisted cord. Thread cord around neck to tie at center front.

Cardigan
Left front
** Using No. 7 (5mm) needles cast on 32[34:36] sts.
1st row P1[2:1], K2, *P2, K2, rep from * to last 1[2:1] sts, P1[2:1].
2nd row K1[2:1], P2, *K2, P2, rep from * to last 1[2:1] sts, K1[2:1].
Rep these 2 rows for 5½in (4cm), ending with a 2nd row.
Next row P1[2:1], K2, *yo, P2 tog, K2, rep from * to last 1[2:1] sts, P1[2:1].
Rib 3 more rows, increasing one st at center of last row, 33[35:37] sts.
Change to No. 9 (6mm) needles and cont in stockinette st as follows:
Work 6[8:10] rows. **
Shape front edge
Next row K to last 2 sts, K2 tog.
Cont to dec in this way at end of every foll 10th row until 29[31:33] sts rem. Work 7[5:3] rows straight.
Mark end of last row to denote beg of armhole.
Shape raglan armhole
Next row Sl1, K1, psso, K to end.
Next row P to last 2 sts, P2 tog tbl.
2nd size only
Rep last 2 rows once more.
3rd size only
Rep last 2 rows twice more.
All sizes
1st row Sl1, K1, psso, K to last 2 sts, K2 tog.
2nd row P to end.
3rd row Sl1, K1, psso, K to end.
4th row P to end.
5th to 10th rows Work rows 3 and 4 three times.
Rep these 10 rows 3 times more.
K tog the 3 rem sts and fasten off.

Right front
Work as given for left front from ** to **
Shape front edge
Next row Sl1, K1, psso, K to end.
Cont to dec in this way at beg of every foll 10th row until 29[31:33] sts rem. Work 7[5:3] rows straight. Mark beg of last row to denote start of armhole.

Shape raglan armhole
Next row K to last 2 sts, K2 tog.
Next row P2 tog, P to end.
2nd size only
Rep last 2 rows once more.

3rd size only
Rep last 2 rows twice more.
All sizes
Complete to match left front reversing shapings.

Cardigan back
Using No. 7 (5mm) needles cast on 68[72:76] sts.
1st row P1, K2, *P2, K2, rep from * to last st, P1.
2nd row K1, P2, *K2, P2, rep from * to last st, K1.
Rep these 2 rows for 5½in (14cm), ending with a 2nd row.

Coral Mula

Brian Mayor

Technique tip
Working short rows
This is a form of shaping widely used to achieve a graduated edge.
The collar on the sweater is worked in rows from one front edge around to the other. The neck edge is shorter than the outer edge of the collar, and in order to achieve this shaping the pattern includes short rows at regular intervals.

To produce a short row you work to within the last two stitches of the row, turn and leave these two stitches un-worked.

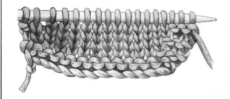

Work to the end of the row. You will see that this forms more rows on the right-hand edge of the fabric than on the left.

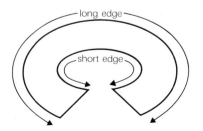

This shaping occurs evenly throughout the collar so that the left-hand edge has fewer rows than the right-hand edge, so forming a circular shape.

Next row P1, K2, *yo, P2 tog, K2, rep from * to last st, P1.
Rib 3 more rows increasing one st at the center on the last row.
69[73:77] sts.
With No. 9 (6mm) needles cont in stockinette st until back is same length as front up to beg of armhole shaping. End with P row. Mark each end of last row to denote beg of armholes.
Shape raglan armholes
Next row Sl1, K1, psso, K to last 2 sts, K2 tog.
1st size only
Next row P2 tog, P to last 2 sts, P2 tog tbl.
2nd size only

Rep last 2 rows once more.
3rd size only
Rep last 2 rows twice more.
All sizes
Next row Sl1, K1, psso, K to last 2 sts, K2 tog.
Next row P to end.
Rep last 2 rows until 21 sts rem, ending with a P row. Bind off.

Left sleeve
*** Using No. 7 (5mm) needles cast on 32[34:34] sts.
1st row P1[2:2], K2, *P2, K2, rep from * to last 1[2:2] sts, P1[2:2].
2nd row K1[2:2], P2, *K2, P2, rep from * to last 1[2:2] sts, K1[2:2].

Rep these 2 rows for 4in (10cm); end with a 2nd row. Change to No. 9 (6mm) needles.
Next row K1[2:1], now K into front and back of each st to last 2[3:2] sts, K to end. 61[63:65] sts.
Beg with P row, cont in stockinette st until sleeve measures 17¼in (44cm) from beg; end with a P row. Mark each end of last row to denote start of raglan shaping.
Shape raglan armholes
1st row Sl1, K1, psso, K to last 2 sts, K2 tog.
2nd row P2 tog, P to last 2 sts, P2 tog tbl. Rep 1st and 2nd rows twice more.
Next row As first row.
Next row P to end.
Rep last 2 rows until 13 sts remain, ending with a P row. ***
Shape for neck
1st row Sl1, K1, psso, K5, bind off rem 6 sts. Cut off yarn. Turn and rejoin yarn to rem sts.
2nd row P2 tog, P to end.
3rd row Sl1, K1, psso, K2, K2 tog.
4th row P2 tog, P1.
K tog the 2 rem sts and fasten off.

Right sleeve
Work as given for left sleeve from *** to ***.
Shape for neck
1st row Bind off 6 sts, K to last 2 sts, K2 tog.
Complete to match left sleeve, reversing shaping.

Button border
Join raglan seams. Mark center back neck. With RS facing join yarn to center back neck and with No. 7 (5mm) needles pick up and K 13 sts along back neck, 11 sts along left sleeve top, and K 9 sts for each 10 row-ends along left front edge to top of ribbing and 30 sts evenly along top edge of ribbing.
1st row K1, *P1, K1, rep from * to end.
2nd row K2, *P1, K1, rep from * to last st, K1.
Rep these 2 rows 3 times more. Bind off in ribbing.

Buttonhole border
With RS facing join yarn to lower edge of right front and with No. 7 (5mm) needles pick up and K sts as left side; end at center back neck. Rib 3 rows.
Buttonhole row Rib 3, *yo, K2 tog, rib 6, rep from * twice more, yo, K2 tog, rib to end.
Rib 4 more rows. Bind off in ribbing.

To finish
Do not press. Join borders. Sew on the buttons.
Cord
Using four 4½yd (4.5m) lengths of yarn together make a twisted cord and thread through holes at waist.

Serge Krouglikoff

94

EXTRA SPECIAL Sewing

Easy lines

There are no fitting problems with this blouson dress or tunic — simply adjust the drawstring and it fits any size from 10 to 16. The dress has a large softly rolled collar and topstitching to pick out the shape of the sleeve cap.

Gary Warren

Measurements
To fit sizes 10 to 16.
Shoulder to hem length, 48¾in (123cm).
Tunic version length, 36⅝in (93cm).

Suggested fabrics
Either garment may be made in any
soft fabric which will drape well. Viyella®
or other wool/cotton or synthetic blends,
brushed cotton, fine velvet or pinwale
corduroy would all be suitable.
Experienced dressmakers could make the
dress in silk.

Materials
Dress: 5½yd (5m) of 36in (90cm) or
  45in (115cm) - wide fabric
Tunic: 4⅞yd (4.4m) of 36in (90cm) -
  wide fabric
2yd (1.8m) of 1in (2.5cm) - wide
  matching seam binding
Matching thread
Matching or contrasting buttonhole
  twist
Tailor's chalk
Yardstick
Flexible curve
Dressmaker's graph paper.

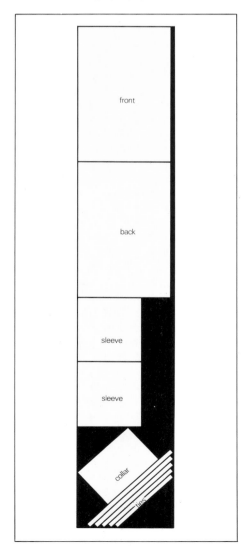

Dress

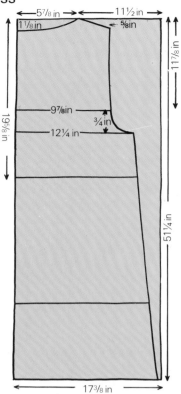

1 For the front, cut a piece of fabric 34⅝in
(88cm) wide by 51¼in (130cm) long.
Fold the fabric in half lengthwise and pin
around edges. Mark out the pattern shape
on the fabric following the measurements
on the diagram, using a flexible curve,
yardstick and tailor's chalk. Cut out.
Repeat for the back section.
2 For the collar, cut a bias strip of fabric
27¼×16in (69.5×40cm). You
may find it easier to cut the shapes from
dressmaker's graph paper first.

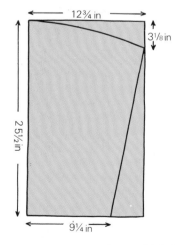

3 For the sleeves, cut two pieces of fabric
25½in (65cm) square. Fold each piece in
half lengthwise and pin the edges
together. Mark out the pattern shape on
the fabric following the diagram, using a
flexible curve, yardstick and tailor's chalk.
Cut out.

4 For the tie belt, cut $1\frac{5}{8}$in (4cm)-wide bias strips to make a total length of $2\frac{3}{4}$yd (2.5m). For the cuff ties, cut enough $1\frac{5}{8}$in (4cm)-wide bias strips to make two ties, each 24in (60cm) long.

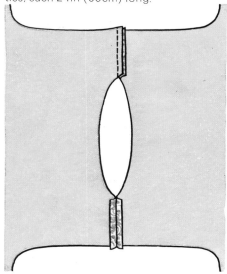

5 Pin, baste and stitch the shoulder seams, with right sides together and raw edges even. Press the seams open.

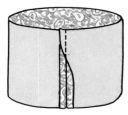

6 Match short ends of collar. Pin, baste and stitch. Press seams open.

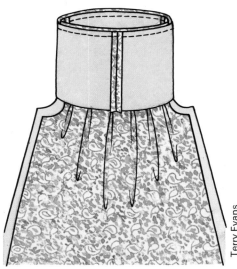

7 Match one long edge of the collar to the raw edge of the neck, right sides together, positioning the seam at the center of the back. Pin, baste and stitch. Clip seam allowances of neck and press upward.

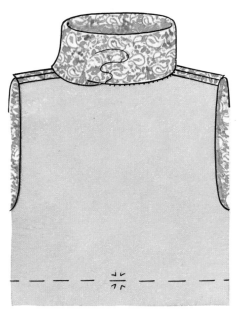

8 To finish the collar, fold it in half, turning it to the inside of the dress. Turn under and press the seam allowance along the free edge of the collar. Slip stitch this folded edge to the dress along the line of machine stitching as shown, so that the stitching does not show on the right side.

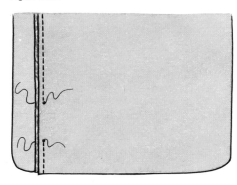

9 Pin, baste and stitch the side seams of the dress with right sides together and raw edges matching. In the same way, pin, baste and stitch the side seams of each sleeve. Leave a $\frac{5}{8}$in (1.5cm) opening $\frac{3}{4}$in (2cm) in from the raw cuff edge of each sleeve, through which to thread the cuff tie later. Press seams open.

10 Mark the waistline of the dress with a line of basting stitches, and mark the center front of the dress with a tailor's tack. The waistline should be 20½in (52cm) from the shoulder seam, where it meets the neck edge, and should follow the grain of the fabric. (You can vary the position to suit your figure.)

11 At the waistline, working on the right side, measure 1⅜in (3.5cm) to each side of the center point. Mark these points and make a pair of vertical buttonholes, ¾in (2cm) deep, by hand or machine.

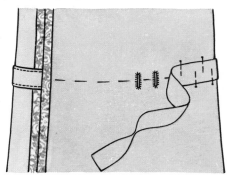

12 On the wrong side, pin the seam binding tape in position over the line of basting, with the basting centered under it, starting at one of the side seams. Baste and stitch close to the edges of the tape to form a casing for the tie belt, being careful to keep the stitching straight.

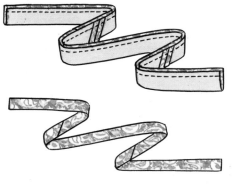

13 For the tie belt, join the bias strips to make a 1¾yd (1.5m) length. Fold it in half right sides together, and stitch down one long edge. Turn the strip right side out by pulling it through one end. Thread the belt through the casing and knot each end.

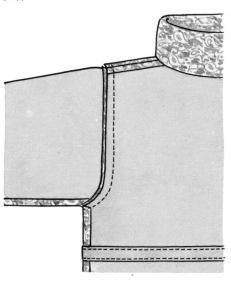

14 Pin, baste and stitch the sleeves to the armholes with right sides together, matching underarm seams. Clip the seam allowances at underarm curves. Press the seam allowances toward the sleeves. Turn the dress right side out and top stitch around the armholes.

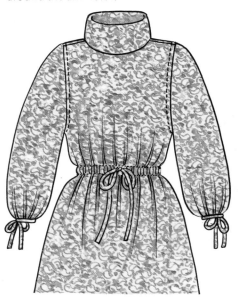

15 Turn in ¼in (6mm) along the wrist edges of the sleeves and baste. Turn up another ⅝in (1.5cm) and stitch close to both folds to make a casing. Make the cuff ties, thread them through the sleeve and knot the ends, as on the tie belt.

16 Turn up and stitch ¼in (6mm) around hem of dress. Try on dress to check length. Turn up a further 1¾in (4.5cm) all around and hem by hand.

Tunic

The tunic is made in the same way as the dress; the only difference is that the front and back pieces measure 34½in (88cm) wide by 39½in (100cm) long.

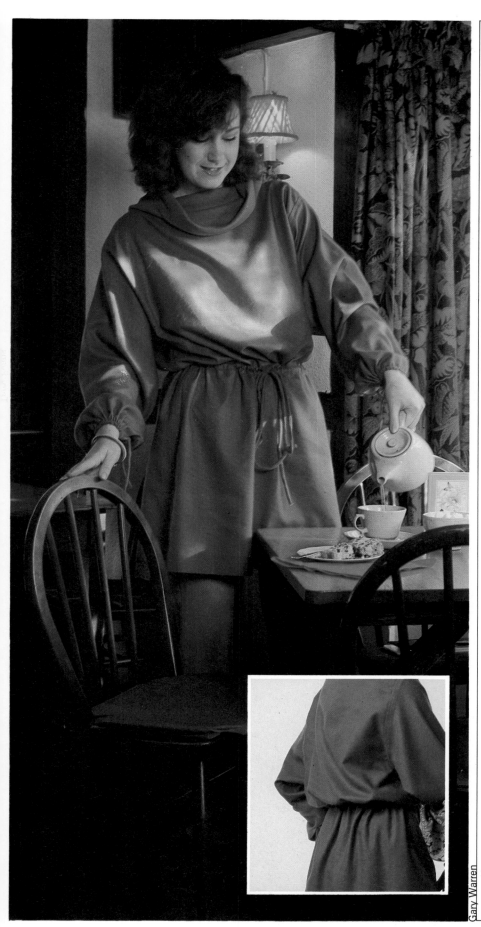

Technique tip
Cutting a collar on the bias

Although it takes up more fabric than a straight-cut collar, a bias-cut collar like the one on this dress will fit the neckline more easily and will fold more naturally.

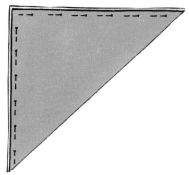

After cutting the main pattern pieces, trim the remaining fabric to make a piece 36in (90cm) square. Fold one raw edge diagonally to match one selvage. Pin the edges together as shown.

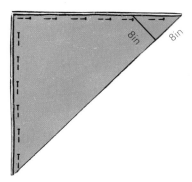

Mark a point on the fold 8in (20cm) in from one of the corners (i.e. half the width of the collar piece). Using tailor's chalk, draw a line 8in (20cm) long, perpendicular to the fold of the fabric to meet the edge of the triangle of fabric.

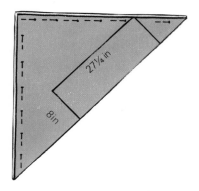

Starting from this second point, draw another line, parallel to the fold in the fabric, measuring $27\frac{1}{4}$in (69.5cm). Now draw another 8in (20cm) line joining the line to fold. Pin around lines and cut out.

EXTRA SPECIAL Sewing

Baby Smocks

Hand-smocked baby clothes are expensive to buy but, fortunately, simple to make. A few remnants of printed cotton, carefully smocked, can be made into an endearing little dress for a special occasion. We've made two versions of the dress—one a "patchwork" of three different fabrics, the other a trimmed version in a single fabric.

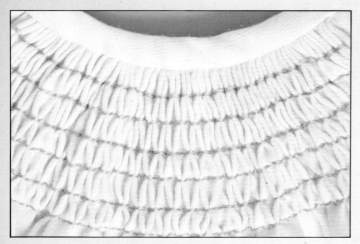

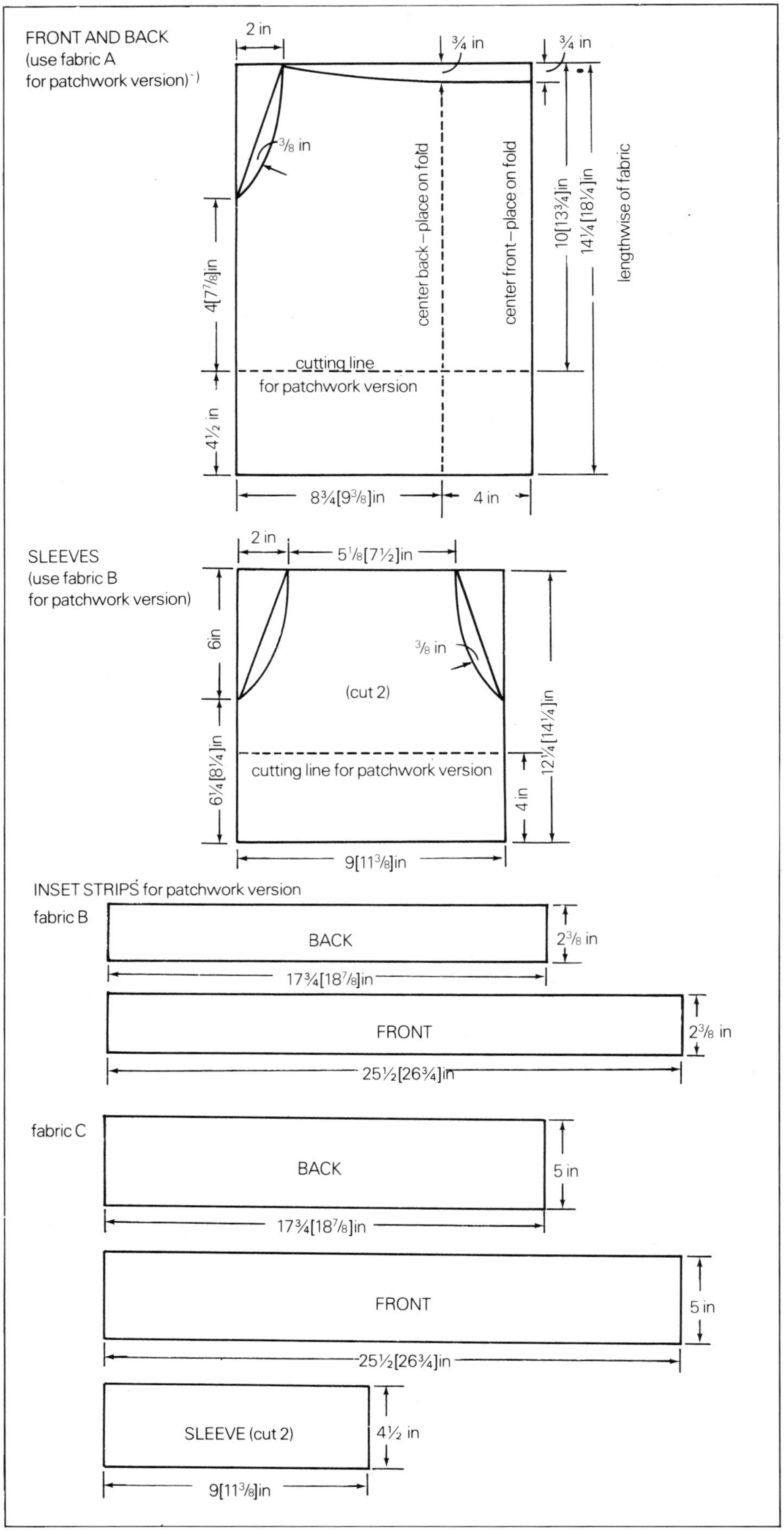
FRONT AND BACK
(use fabric A
for patchwork version)
2 in
¾ in
¾ in
⅜ in
center back – place on fold
center front – place on fold
10[13¾]in
14¼[18¼]in
lengthwise of fabric
4[7⅞]in
cutting line
for patchwork version
4½ in
8¾[9⅜]in
4 in
SLEEVES
(use fabric B
for patchwork version)
2 in
5⅛[7½]in
6in
⅜ in
(cut 2)
12¼[14¼]in
6¼[8¼]in
cutting line for patchwork version
4 in
9[11⅜]in
INSET STRIPS for patchwork version
fabric B
BACK
2⅜ in
17¾[18⅞]in
FRONT
2⅜ in
25½[26¾]in
fabric C
BACK
5 in
17¾[18⅞]in
FRONT
5 in
25½[26¾]in
SLEEVE (cut 2)
4½ in
9[11⅜]in

Measurements

To fit ages 1-1½, 1½-2 years.
Finished length 11¼[15¼]in (28.5 [38.5]cm).
⅝in (1.5cm) seam allowances and 1¾in (4.5cm) hem allowance are included.
Note Measurements are given for the smaller size. Figures in brackets [] are for the larger size. Where only one figure is given, this applies to both sizes.

Suggested fabrics

The patchwork dress is made in printed cotton, and the trimmed dress is made in a cotton and wool blend. Brushed cotton, synthetics, or synthetic/cotton blends would also be suitable.

Materials

For the patchwork version—using 36in (90cm)-wide fabric:
¾[⅞]yd (.6[.8]m) fabric A (for back and front)
½[⅝]yd (.4[.5]m) fabric B (for upper sleeve and upper hem)
½yd (.4m) of fabric C (for lower hem and lower sleeve)
Matching sewing thread
Cotton embroidery floss for smocking
Length of transfer gathering dots—approx. ⅜in (1cm) spacing
Small button
12in (30cm) ¼in (6mm)-wide elastic
Flexible curve, yardstick, tailor's chalk

For the plain version:
1¼[1⅝]yd (1.10[1.40]m) 36in (90cm)-wide fabric or ⅞[1⅛]yd (.8[1]m) 45in (115cm)-wide fabric
3⅓yd (3.00m) of ⅝in (1.5cm)-wide émbroidered ribbon
Other materials as for patchwork dress

Patchwork dress

1 For the front of the dress, cut out a rectangle 10[13¾]in (25[35]cm) by 25½[26¾]in (65[68]cm) from fabric A. Fold the fabric in half widthwise and pin the edges to prevent their slipping. Mark and cut out shape for the front as shown in the measurement diagram, using a yardstick, tailor's chalk and a flexible curve. For the armhole seams, draw a diagonal; then, using a flexible curve, draw a curved line inside the diagonal. Also, cut a strip of fabric B, 2⅜in (6cm) by 25½[26¾]in (65[68]cm) for the upper hem section and a strip of fabric C, 5in (12.5cm) by 25½[26¾]in (65[68]cm) for the lower hem section.
2 For the back of the dress, cut a rectangle 10[13¾]in (25[35]cm) by 17½[18¾]in (45[48]cm) from fabric A. Fold the fabric in half widthwise and pin and cut out the shape as for the front of the dress, following the appropriate measurements on the diagram. Also cut a strip of fabric B, 2⅜in (6cm) by 17½[18¾]in (45[48]cm) for the upper hem section and a strip of

John Hutchinson

fabric C, 5in (12.5cm) by 17½[18¾]in (45[48]cm) for the lower hem section.

3 For the sleeves, cut out two rectangles of fabric B, each 12¼[14¼]in (31[36]cm) by 9[11⅜]in (23[29]cm). Cut out the shapes for the sleeves following the measurement diagram. For the cuffs, cut two strips of fabric C, each 4½in (11.5cm) by 9[11⅜]in (23[29]cm). For the cuff casing, cut two strips of fabric C, each 9[11⅜]in (23[29]cm) by 1⅛in (3cm).

4 For the neck binding, cut a bias strip of fabric A, 1⅝in (4cm) by 12in (30cm).

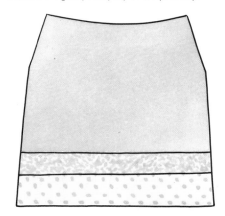

5 Next, join the patchwork sections to make the front, back and sleeves. Use French seams for a neat, strong finish. Pin, baste and stitch upper hem sections to front and back sections, and attach lower hem sections to upper hem section. Attach cuff sections to sleeves. Press each seam after you stitch it.

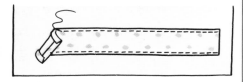

6 Turn under the short ends of the casing strips ⅝in (1.5cm). Turn under ¼in (6mm) along the long edges and stitch. Baste the strips to the wrong side of the cuff sections, placing the lower edges 1in (2.5cm) above the raw edges of the cuffs and the short ends an equal distance from each side of the cuffs. Machine stitch close to the casing edges.

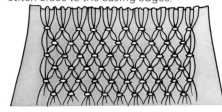

7 Cut the smocking dot transfer strip ⅛in (3cm) shorter than the width of the bodice and 2in (5cm) deep. Iron the dots onto the front bodice section and smock the dress as shown in the Technique tips.

Technique tips

Marking and gathering for smocking

Smocking is a decorative stitch worked over evenly gathered fabric. The easiest way to mark the fabric and ensure that the markings are evenly spaced is to use an iron-on transfer of smocking dots. These are available in a range of sizes—for this dress, dots spaced about ⅜in (1cm) apart are used.

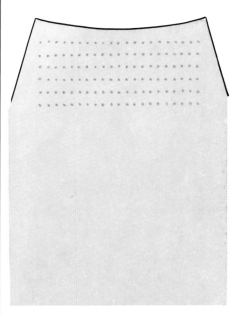

Cut a strip of dots ⅝in (1.5cm) shorter than the width of the bodice. Six rows of dots are sufficient—for this dress you must use an even number. Iron the grid on the front of the dress.

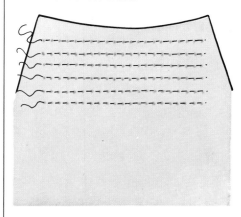

Run six lines of gathering thread through the smocking, taking each stitch just under one dot. Pull up the threads so the area to be smocked is 12in (30cm) narrower than it was before gathering, and tie the ends.

Honeycomb stitch for smocking

Thread a needle with the embroidery floss. Starting at the top left-hand corner of the bodice as you look at it, make a small back stitch through the first dot, bringing the needle out to the left of the dot.

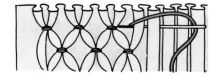

Next, move the needle a little to the right and take a stitch under the second dot and back under the first dot, drawing the two dots together.

Take the needle to the right again; insert it behind the second dot in almost the same place as before and bring it out of the fabric in the row below, just to the left of the second dot.

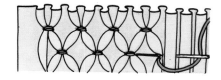

Take the needle to the right, make a small stitch under the third dot in the second row, then under the second dot again and draw the dots together.

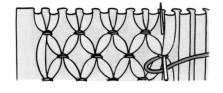

Take the needle back to the third dot, insert it as shown, and bring it out just to the left of the third dot in the first row. Continue this pattern of stitches along the first two rows. Repeat the process over the next two pairs of rows. This stitch is particularly suitable for children's clothes, as there is plenty of ease in it.

Terry Evans

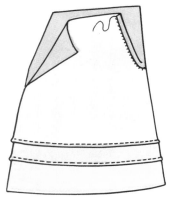

8 Mark center back of neck and measure 5in (12.5cm) down from this point. Cut a slit this length for center back opening. Finish the raw edges with a small, hand-rolled hem, tapering to the end of the slit.

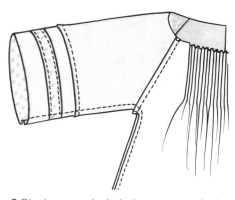

9 Pin, baste and stitch sleeves to armhole edges of front and back sections, matching the curved edges and using French seams. Press seams.

10 Pin and baste underarm and side seams, matching seams at underarm points. Starting from wrist, stitch underarm and side seams (again using French seams), pivoting fabric around needle at underarm point to turn corner. Take care not to catch in the edges of the casings.

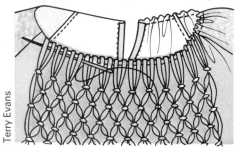

11 Run two gathering threads—by hand—all around top of back, sleeves and front of dress, starting $\frac{1}{4}$in (5mm) from edge of center back opening. When gathering across the smocked area, space the gathering stitches the same distance apart as the gathering stitches of the smocking, so that the "tubes" of fabric formed by the smocking run in unbroken lines up to the neck. Draw up gathering

threads so that the neck measures 10in (26cm) all around, distributing the gathers evenly.

12 Turn under and press $\frac{1}{4}$in (5mm) along one long edge of the bias strip. Pin and baste this binding to neck edge of dress. Turn back the binding as shown and, working on the right side, slip stitch it to the dress, making one tiny stitch into each "tube" of smocked fabric. Turn binding to inside, turn under $\frac{1}{4}$in (5mm) and slip stitch this folded edge to inside of neck.

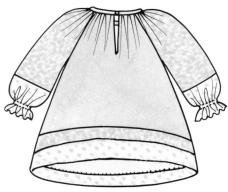

13 Stitch button to left side of neck opening and work a thread loop, as in the Technique tip, on the right side.
14 Turn under and stitch $\frac{1}{4}$in (5mm) double hems on each cuff. Insert 6in (15cm) lengths of elastic into casings.

Measure the baby's wrist and shorten elastic if necessary, leaving a $\frac{1}{4}$in (5mm) overlap. Sew ends of elastic together.
15 At the hem edge, turn up and stitch a $\frac{1}{4}$in (5mm) hem, then turn up a further 1$\frac{5}{8}$in (4cm). Baste and hand-hem the finished edge in place close to seam joining upper and lower hem sections.

Plain dress

1 For the front of the dress, cut out a rectangle of fabric 25$\frac{1}{2}$[26$\frac{3}{4}$]in (65[68]cm) wide by 14$\frac{1}{4}$[18$\frac{1}{4}$]in (36.5 [46.5]cm) long and fold in half. Pin around raw edges and mark and cut out front section, following the measurement diagram.
2 Cut a rectangle 17$\frac{1}{2}$[18$\frac{3}{4}$]in (45[48] cm) wide by 14$\frac{1}{4}$[18$\frac{1}{4}$]in (36.5[46.5] cm) long for the back and two rectangles 12$\frac{1}{4}$[14$\frac{1}{4}$]in (31[36]cm) by 9[11$\frac{3}{8}$]in (23[29]cm) for the sleeves. Cut out the back and sleeves, following the diagram.
3 Cut out a bias strip 1$\frac{5}{8}$in (4cm) by 12in (30cm) for the neck edge. Cut two strips 9 [11$\frac{3}{8}$]in (23[29]cm) by 1$\frac{1}{8}$in (3cm) for the cuff casings.
4 Make and smock the dress as directed in steps 6-13 for the patchwork dress.
5 Mark the position of the trimming on the hem and sleeves of the dress. Run two lines of basting stitches around the bottom of the dress 3$\frac{1}{4}$in (8.5cm) and 4in (10cm) from the raw edge. Run lines of basting stitches around the sleeves, 4in (10cm) above the raw edges of the cuffs.
6 Cut 2 lengths of lace and ribbon to fit around the hem and one for each wrist, allowing $\frac{5}{8}$in (1.5cm) for joining. Hand-sew ribbon in place along basting.
7 Turn up hems and gather wrists as for the patchwork dress, steps 14 and 15.

Technique tip

Thread loops

These are useful substitutes for button-holes and can be used where you do not have an overlap of fabric, as on this baby dress.

Position the loop close to the top of the neck opening. Using double thread, make a tiny back stitch near the top of the opening. (The thread ends are trimmed after the loop is completed.) Bring the

needle down along the edge the same distance as the diameter of the button. Make a small stitch on the edge. Make a second stitch at the upper position and a third at the lower position so that the loop is made up of six strands of thread.

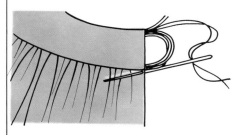

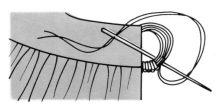

Starting from the bottom of the loop, work loop stitch as shown (similar to buttonhole or blanket stitch) all around the strands of the loop.

Terry Evans

Top fashion

This easy-fitting casual top has dropped shoulders and an elasticized waist. Topstitched pockets are set into the side seams and trimmed with bias binding to match the neckline. The topstitching is echoed on the turnback cuffs, and an embroidered motif adds an individual look.

Measurements

Measurements are given for size 10; sizes 12 to 16 are given in brackets []. Where only one measurement is given, this applies to all sizes.

Materials

2yd (1.8) of 54/60in (140/150cm)-wide fabric or 2⅝yd (2.6cm) of 36in (90cm)-wide fabric

1¾yd (1.6m) of 1in (2.5cm)-wide seam binding

1⅛yd (1m) elastic ⅝in (1.5cm) wide

1¾yd (1.2m) of 1in (2.5cm)-wide seam binding

Two ⅝in (1.5cm) buttons, embroidery hoop, matching thread, flexible curve, tailor's chalk

1 For front section, cut one rectangle (see page 106). Fold in half lengthwise, pin the edges even and, using tailor's chalk, draw pattern shape on fabric. Keeping the fabric folded, cut out the front section. Remove pins. Repeat for back. Work embroidered motif in position shown.

2 Cut out four pocket pieces following the diagram and using flexible curve. Cut out two sleeve pieces. Sew lines of basting to mark cuff foldlines, 3¾in (9.5cm) and 6¾in (17cm) from one long edge. On back and front baste lines to mark shoulder and waistline (see diagram). Mark pocket positions.

3 Pin, baste and stitch bias binding to front and back neck with right sides together, starting at one shoulder edge. Turn to inside and slip stitch in place. Fold in ¼in (5mm) hem on binding ends.

Measurement diagram for top

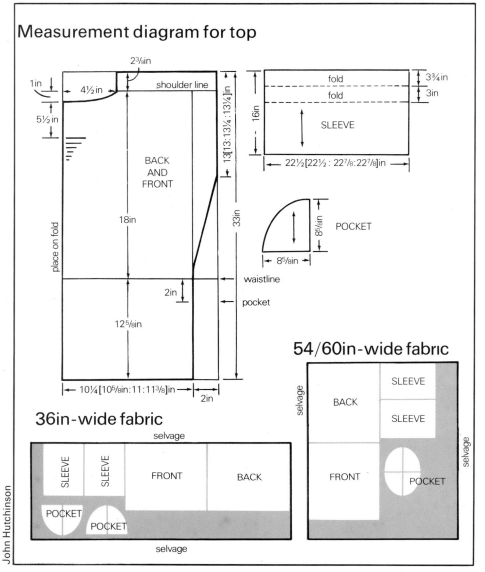

BACK AND FRONT

2³⁄₈in

1in

4½in

shoulder line

5½in

13[13:13¾:13¼]in

18in

33in

place on fold

waistline

2in

pocket

12⁵⁄₈in

10¼[10⁵⁄₈in:11:11³⁄₈]in

2in

SLEEVE

3¾in

3in

fold

fold

16in

22½[22½ : 22⁷⁄₈:22⁷⁄₈]in

POCKET

8⁵⁄₈in

8⁵⁄₈in

36in-wide fabric

selvage

SLEEVE SLEEVE FRONT BACK

POCKET POCKET

selvage

54/60in-wide fabric

selvage

BACK SLEEVE SLEEVE

FRONT POCKET

selvage

John Hutchinson

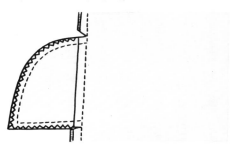

placing right sides together and upper raw edges of pockets 1³⁄₈in (3.5cm) down from marked waistline.

8 Matching raw edges exactly, pin, baste and sew side seams and free edges of pockets. Begin at hem edge and sew until you reach pocket. Pivot machine needle and continue stitching around pocket. Pivot machine needle again at the side seam and continue sewing to the armhole.

9 Clip seam allowances above and below pocket to allow side seam to be pressed open. Finish the short edges where you have clipped the fabric. Zig-zag pocket seam allowances together.

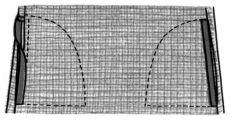

10 Turn garment right side out. With pockets toward center front, baste opening edges together. Press. Remove basting.

11 Cut a length of bias binding to fit one side of each pocket opening, plus allowances for finishing at each end. Fold binding over front pocket edge and slip stitch both folded edges of binding in place on inside and outside of pocket.

12 Baste pocket to front around pocket edges and topstitch in place, following seamline of pocket, pivoting needle at corner.

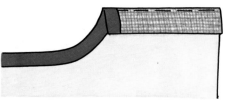

4 Fold each front shoulder edge to inside along basted shoulder line. Pin, baste and press edge.

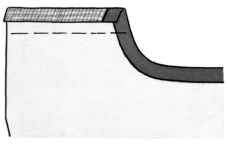

5 Fold each back shoulder facing to inside for ¾in (2cm). Pin, baste, press edge.

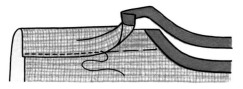

6 Lap each back shoulder over front so that basted shoulder lines are aligned. Pin and baste together. Add a line of topstitching ¼in (5mm) from fold, 4¾in (12cm) long, beginning at shoulder edge.

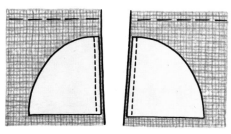

7 Pin, baste and sew one pocket piece to each side edge of back and front pieces,

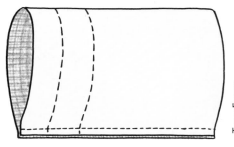

Terry Evans

13 Fold each sleeve in half perpendicular to foldlines, with right sides together and edges matching. Baste and sew sleeve seam. Press seams open and finish seam allowance.

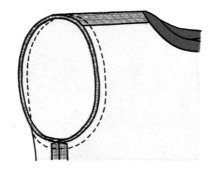

14 Pin, baste and sew each sleeve into armhole, right sides together and underarm seam matching side seam. Press seam allowance toward sleeve and finish by sewing raw edges together.

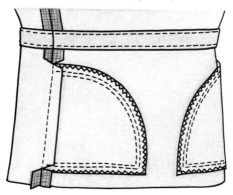

15 Cut a length of seam binding to fit waist of garment, plus allowances for

finishing ends. Starting at one side seam and folding under end of seam binding, baste seam binding centered over marked waistline. Fold under the other short end at side seam. Sew on-to wrong side, close to each edge of tape, to form casing for elastic. Cut a piece of elastic to fit your waist, plus $\frac{3}{4}$in (2cm) overlap. Insert elastic through side opening in casing and join ends.

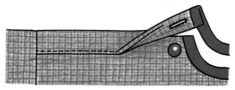

16 Make a buttonhole in the shoulder overlap, near the neck edge, as shown. Sew buttons on underlap to correspond to buttonholes. Slip stitch ends of binding on folded-under edges of neckline to finish.

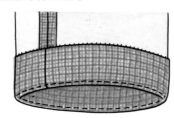

17 Fold under $\frac{1}{4}$in (5mm) to wrong side on sleeve edges and machine-stitch

hem in place. Turn cuffs to the wrong side along the first basted line. Press and topstitch $\frac{1}{4}$in (5mm) from this line to finish the edge of the cuff.

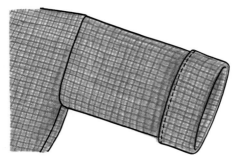

18 Hem inner edge of cuff to sleeve and turn up cuff on right side along second basted line. Press.

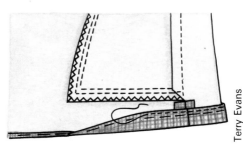

19 Fold under a $\frac{1}{4}$in (5mm) hem to finish lower edge. Turn up a further $1\frac{1}{8}$in (3cm) and machine-stitch. Press.

Terry Evans

Technique tip
Machine embroidery

The motif on the front of the blue shirt is a piece of machine embroidery. It may be done on any zig-zag sewing machine.
If you are using sheer fabric, the motif is easier to sew if you interface it with a piece of fusible interfacing. Trace the pattern from the diagram on the right and transfer it to the center front of the shirt.

Stretch the fabric over an embroidery hoop. Slip the hoop under the foot of the machine. (You may need to remove the foot in order to do this.) Sew the lines in satin stitch, following the pattern.

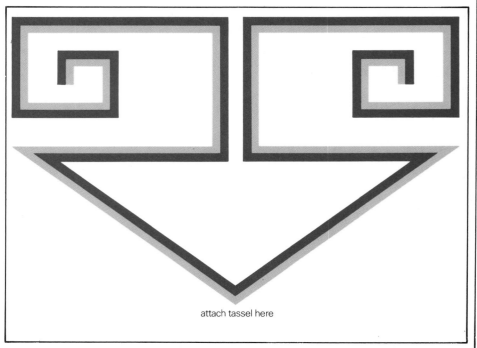

attach tassel here

Brian Mayor

Scenic knitted pillow covers

Bring the seaside back home with this nostalgic set of three knitted pillow covers.

Size
16in square

Materials
Working in knitting worsted; this set of covers requires:
10oz (275g) in sky blue
4oz (100g) in sea blue
3oz (75g) in emerald green
3oz (75g) in olive green
2oz (50g) in dark green
2oz (50g) in ocher
1oz (25g) in red
1oz (25g) in royal blue
1oz (25g) in beige
1oz (25g) in rust
1oz (25g) in off-white
1oz (25g) in dark brown
1oz (25g) in sage green
Scraps of pink and white yarn
1 pair No. 4 (3¾mm) needles
Large-eyed embroidery needle
3 x 12in (30cm) zippers
3 x 16in (40cm) square pillow forms

Gauge
24 sts and 32 rows to 4in (10cm) in pattern.

Note
The fronts of the covers are worked from charts, with each square representing one stitch. When following the charts, read all knit rows from right to left and all purl rows from left to right. Use separate balls of yarn for each main area of color, twisting yarns when changing color to avoid leaving a hole in the finished work. Introduce each new color as it is needed, cutting off after completing each color area. You may want to wind a few small balls of some colors for the smaller color areas. When a color is separated by only a few stitches of another color in a row, it should be carried across the back of the work until it is needed again; if the yarn has to pass over five stitches or more, link it in at center back of the section. Be careful not to pull the color not in use too tightly.

Pillow cover 1 (page 111)
Using No. 4 (3¾mm) needles and sea blue cast on 96 sts for lower edge of front. K1 row.

Beginning at row 1 of chart 1, with a P row, work from chart until 130 rows have been worked, so completing the front. Proceed in stripes for back: work 56 rows sky blue, 27 rows emerald green, 2 rows olive green, 5 rows ocher and 40 rows sea blue. Bind off.

To finish
Using the large-eyed embroidery needle and some white yarn, embroider a seagull in top right-hand corner, following chart 1, by the duplicate stitch method (see Knitting Course 10, Volume 2, page 38). Next, thread some red yarn and embroider the roofs of the beige villas, using the same method. Repeat this technique to embroider the roofs of the off-white villas in pink yarn. Secure all ends and cut off yarn.
Block according to yarn. Darn in all loose ends on the wrong side of the work, but do not cut these. With right sides together join seams leaving lower edge open. Join 2in (5cm) from each corner along lower edge. Insert one 12in (30cm) zipper. Fill the cover with one 16in (40cm) pillow form and close the zipper.

Pillow cover 2 (page 112)
Using No. 4 (3¾mm) needles and ocher, cast on 96 sts for lower edge of front. K1 row. Beginning at row 1 of chart 2 with a P row, work from chart until 130 rows have been worked, so completing the front. Proceed in stripes for back as follows: work 56 rows of sky blue, 26 rows of emerald green, 2 rows of rust; 5 rows of ocher, 29 rows of sea blue and 11 rows of ocher. Bind off.

To finish
Using the large-eyed embroidery needle and some pink yarn, embroider the roofs of the off-white villas, following chart 2, and using duplicate stitch. Thread some red yarn and embroider the roofs of the beige villas, using the same method. Repeat this technique to embroider the beach umbrellas on the distant shoreline in red and blue yarn. Now with some white yarn embroider two seagulls in the top left-hand corner of the pillow front and embroider the ripples at the water's edge. Secure all ends and cut off yarn. Block according to yarn. Darn in all loose

ends on the wrong side of the work, but do not cut these. With right sides together join seams leaving lower edge open. Join 2in (5cm) from each corner along edge, then insert 12in (30cm) zipper. Fill the cover with one 16in (40cm) pillow form and close the zipper. The second pillow of the set is now complete.

Pillow cover 3 (page 113)
Using No. 4 (3¾mm) needles and olive green cast on 96 sts for lower edge of front. K1 row.

Beginning at row 1 of chart 3 with a P row, work from chart until 130 rows have been worked, so completing the front. Proceed in stripes for back as follows: work 69 rows sky blue, 16 rows emerald green and 45 rows olive green. Bind off.

To finish
Using the large-eyed embroidery needle and some pink yarn, embroider the villa roofs, following chart 1, and using duplicate stitch. Secure the ends, and cut off the yarn.

Block according to yarn. Darn in all loose ends on the wrong side of the work, but do not cut. With right sides together, join seams leaving lower edge open. Join 2in (5cm) from each corner along lower edge, then insert 12in (30cm) zipper. Fill the cover with one 16in (40cm) pillow orm and close the zipper. The third scenic pillow knitted is now complete. Line the pillows up at the back of your sofa, or place them in a row on your window seat, then relax and dream about your tropical vacation.

CHART 1

CHART 2

SKY BLUE

DARK GREEN

EMERALD GREEN

OLIVE GREEN

BEIGE

OFF WHITE

RUST

SEA BLUE

RED

ROYAL BLUE

OCHER

WHITE

CHART 3

SKY BLUE

DARK GREEN

RUST

SAGE GREEN

EMERALD GREEN

OFF WHITE

OLIVE GREEN

OCHER

David Laraman

Homemaker

Matching bathroom accessories

This coordinated set of accessories will add style to your bathroom and eliminate clutter at the same time. The set includes a hanging panel with pockets for manicure items, hair cosmetics, comb and brush and bath salts; a lined basket for cotton balls or pretty soap; a tissue box cover; and a quilt-framed mirror.

Sizes
Hanging panel: 17¾in (45cm) deep by 15¾in (40cm) wide. Liner for basket: 6in (15cm) wide by 9in (23cm) long by 2in (5cm) deep.
Tissue box cover: 4¼in (11cm) wide by 4¾in (12cm) long by 5⅛in (13cm) deep.
Quilt-framed mirror: 7 x 9½in (18 x 24cm).
Materials
⅞yd (.8m) of 48in (122cm)-wide
   bold patterned fabric (fabric A)
⅝yd (.5m) of 48in (122cm)-wide
   coordinated fabric (fabric B)
⅝yd (.5m) of 36in (90cm)-wide
   washable synthetic batting
⅞yd (.8m) of 24in (60cm)-wide heavy
   non-woven iron-on interfacing

Gary Warren

2yds (1.8m) of 1in (2.5cm)-wide
   white bias binding
1½yd (1.3m) of 1in (2.5cm)-wide
   white straight seam binding
For hanging panel: 1 bamboo cane,
   15¾in (40cm) long
For lined basket: 1 basket—ours
   measures 6 x 9in (15 x 23cm) at
   the base, 2in (5cm) deep plus a
   handle
For quilt-framed mirror: 1 mirror,
   7 x 9½in (18 x 24cm); 2 pieces
   cardboard, each 7 x 9½in (18 x 24cm);
   and heavy-duty glue
Thread in matching colors

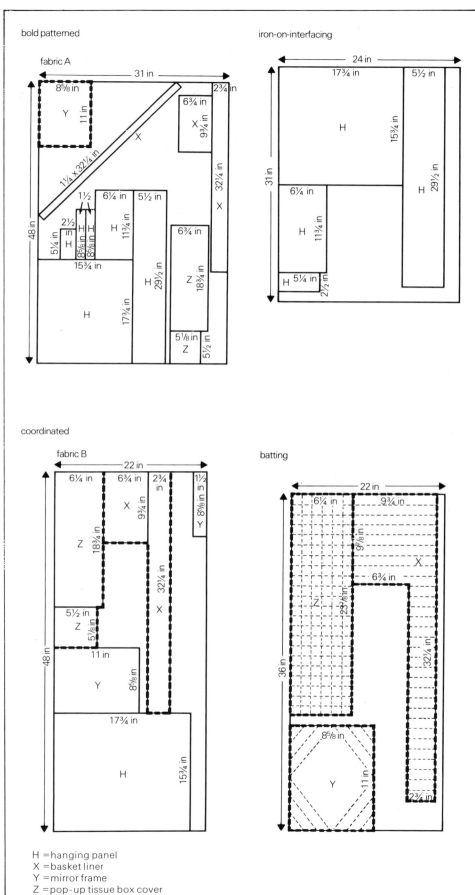

H =hanging panel
X =basket liner
Y =mirror frame
Z =pop-up tissue box cover

Brian Mayor

Hanging panel

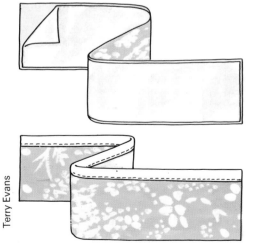

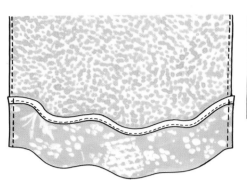

3 Place 29½in (75cm) strip of fabric A wrong side to panel front (fabric B) at lower edge. Pin and baste ends of strip to each panel side and stitch ¼in (5mm) from edges.

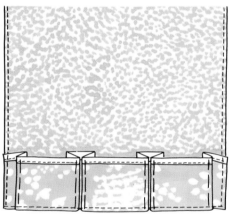

(Use pieces marked "H")

1 For panel back, cut fabric B and interfacing 15¾ x 17¾in (40 x 45cm) and iron interfacing to wrong side of fabric. For panel front, cut fabric A 15¾ x 17¾in (40 x 45cm). With wrong sides together, stitch back to front ⅜in (1cm) from edges all around.

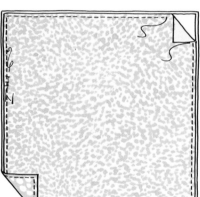

4 Pleat the strip as shown above to make three pockets, each 5⅛in (13cm) wide, taking in 2⅜in (6cm) for pleats at each side and 4¾in (12cm) for each of the two pleats in the center. Baste pleats down folds. Baste pleated strip to lower edge of panel front and stitch ¼in (5mm) from raw edges.

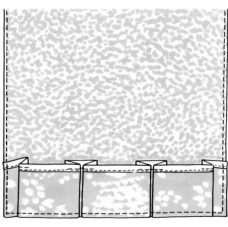

5 Anchor the upper edges of pleats at sides and center by stitching ¼in (5mm) on each side of folds along original stitching line on seam binding. These pockets will take the bulkier items, such as shampoo, talcum powder, hairbrush and bath oil.

2 For pockets, cut strip of fabric A and interfacing 5½ x 29½in (14 x 75cm) and iron interfacing to wrong side of fabric. Bind one long edge with seam binding.

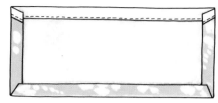

6 For top pockets cut fabric A and interfacing, 6¼ x 11¾in (16 x 30cm), and iron interfacing to wrong side of fabric. Bind one long edge with seam binding. Turn both short sides and other long edges under by ¼in (5mm); baste around edges.

7 Place wrong side of pocket strip on right side of front panel, 4in (10cm) down from top edge and ¾in (2cm) in from left edge. Stitch sides and lower edge to panel.

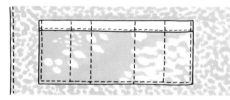

8 To form pockets, add vertical lines of stitching at appropriate intervals to accommodate your nail scissors, emery board, nail polish, hair conditioner, comb, or anything else you need a home for.

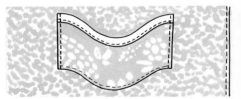

9 For the hair spray holder, cut fabric A and interfacing, 2½ x 5¼in (6.5 x 13.5cm), and iron interfacing to wrong side of fabric. Bind one long edge with seam binding. Turn under ¼in (5mm) on the other long edge. Stitch. Turn under ⅜in (1cm) on the short edges and topstitch these edges to panel, to the right of the upper pockets, forming a loop large enough for a small can of hairspray.

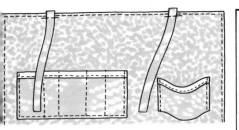

10 For the hangers, cut two strips, $1\frac{1}{2}$ x $8\frac{5}{8}$in (4 x 22cm), from fabric A. With right sides together, stitch long edges. Turn strips right side out; press. Pin one end of each hanger in position, raw edges together, to top of panel, $2\frac{3}{4}$in (7.5cm) from each side.

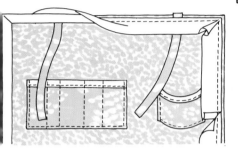

11 Open out bias binding and place one edge along raw edge of panel front. Stitch all around along fold of binding, turning back the binding at the ends to make a neat overlap at join. Trim away excess fabric from edges and corners. Turn bias binding to panel back and slip stitch in place along prefolded edge.

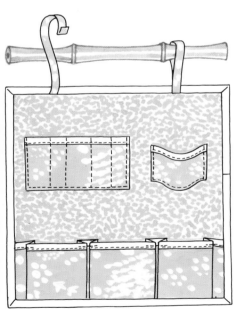

12 Turn under $\frac{1}{4}$in (5mm) at free ends of hangers, then turn under these folded ends another $1\frac{1}{8}$in (3cm) to form a loop to fit over bamboo cane. Slip stitch in position and thread cane through loops. Hang the cane on hooks on the bathroom wall and put your things away.

How to quilt fabric

The lined basket, tissue box cover and mirror all require quilting — a different pattern of quilting for each item. Begin by cutting out the required piece of batting for each item. Do not cut "X" and "Z" pieces into separate components at this point, as it is easier to quilt the fabric first. Then cut corresponding shapes from fabrics following heavy lines. (If your basket measures more than 6 x 9in [15 x 23cm], increase the size of the "X" pieces accordingly.) Place the batting on the wrong side of corresponding fabric pieces and baste across and down the pieces at fairly widely spaced intervals to hold the two layers together. Now stitch — working on the fabric side — using the appropriate pattern.

For the basket liner, stitch parallel lines 1in (2.5cm) apart across width of fabric piece "X." For the mirror frame, stitch lines 1in (2.5cm) apart diagonally to corners of fabric piece "Y," starting at a line drawn across from the center of each side. For the tissue box cover, stitch 1in (2.5cm) squares on fabric piece "Z."

Lined basket

Gary Warren

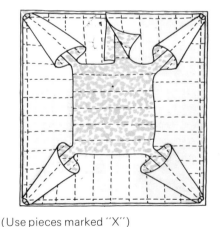

(Use pieces marked "X")

1 From fabric A and quilted fabric B, cut rectangles measuring the same as base of basket, plus $\frac{3}{8}$in (1cm) seam allowance all around. The rectangles marked on the diagram fit a basket base measuring 6 x 9in (15 x 23cm). Cut a long strip from fabric A and quilted fabric B, measuring the same as the distance around the upper edge of basket by depth of basket, plus $\frac{3}{8}$in (1cm) seam allowance all around. (Our basket required a strip $2\frac{3}{4}$ x $32\frac{1}{4}$in [7 x 82cm].) The quilted fabric B forms the inside and fabric A the outside of basket liner.

Terry Evans

2 Make the two sides of the lining separately as follows: place quilted strip on quilted base, right sides together and raw edges even. Turn back $\frac{3}{8}$in (1cm) of the strip at the beginning. Stitch $\frac{3}{8}$in (1cm) from the edge, easing strip to fit base at corners and making two small tucks at each corner, as shown. Place the end of the strip over the turned-back beginning of strip and stitch it in place to form a neat seam.

Repeat these steps with fabric A strip and base pieces to make the underside of the lining.

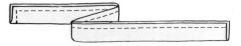

3 Place quilted lining inside the underside piece, wrong sides together. Place in basket and pin together. Check fit and trim excess depth if necessary.

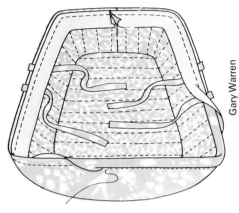

4 If basket has handle, cut four strips of fabric A, $1\frac{1}{4} \times 8\frac{5}{8}$in (3 x 22cm), to make ties. With right sides and raw edges together, stitch along length and one end of each strip, allowing $\frac{3}{8}$in (1cm) seam. Turn right side out and press.

5 Pin unfinished strip ends to raw edge of quilted side of lining, placing them on each side of the handle. Remove lining from basket. Cut a bias strip from fabric A as shown on cutting diagram. Place the strip along the edge of the quilted fabric, right sides together and raw edges even. Baste and stitch through all layers, $\frac{3}{8}$in (1cm) from the edge, incorporating ties and overlapping the ends of the strip as described in Step 2, to make a neat join.

6 Trim excess fabric from raw edge, turn bias strip to underside. Turn under raw edge $\frac{1}{4}$in (5mm) and slip stitch in place.

Mirror

(Use pieces marked "Y")
1 Measure mirror to be used and add $\frac{3}{4}$in (2cm) all around for overhang. Following the diagrams, cut out pieces of quilted fabric of required size. (Our mirror measured 7 x $9\frac{1}{2}$in [18 x 24cm].) This quilted piece will form the mirror frame. Cut out center rectangle piece (measuring $3\frac{1}{2}$ x 6in [9 x 15cm] for our frame).

2 Cut two pieces of cardboard to the same size as the mirror and cut out the center of one of the pieces leaving a frame

1in (2.5cm) wide on all sides. Lay this frame on the wrong side of quilted frame fabric, so that the fabric overhangs $\frac{3}{4}$in (2cm) all around on both inside and outside edges. Snip inside corners of quilted fabric up to cardboard corners. Fold quilting over to inside of cardboard edges and glue in place. Leave outer edges of fabric free.

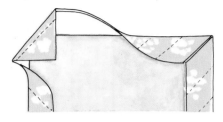

3 Place right side of mirror to wrong side of frame. Fold fabric covers over mirror corners at back and glue. Fold fabric edges over mirror edges, mitering corners and glue firmly to the mirror back as shown.
4 To finish back of frame mirror cut piece of fabric B to same size as quilted fabric A. Lay second piece of cardboard on wrong side of fabric B piece, so that $\frac{3}{4}$in (2cm) of fabric extends on all sides. Wrap fabric over cardboard, corners first, in the same way as for the frame, and glue firmly.

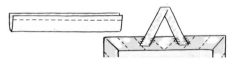

5 For hanger, cut a strip $1\frac{1}{2}$ x $8\frac{5}{8}$in (4 x 22cm) from fabric B. With right sides and raw edges together, stitch lengthwise $\frac{1}{4}$in (5mm) from edge. Turn and press. Hand stitch two ends of loop to the upper edge of the fabric at back of mirror, working back and forth several times to anchor the ends securely.

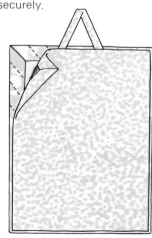

6 Glue covered cardboard back to the back of the framed mirror, concealing the cardboard.

118

Tissue box cover

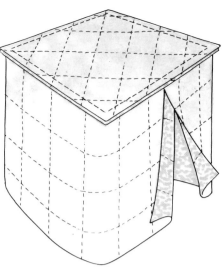

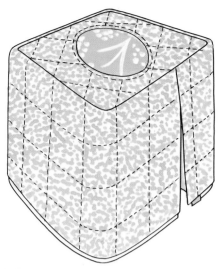

5 Turn lining to inside through oval hole. Topstitch around oval $\frac{1}{4}$in (5mm) from folded edge.

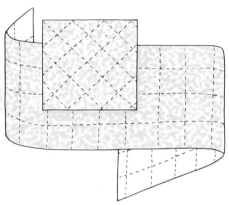

(Use pieces marked "Z")
1 Following cutting diagrams, cut two pieces of quilted fabric B: one measuring $6\frac{1}{4}$ x $18\frac{3}{4}$in (16 x 48cm) for sides; the other, $5\frac{1}{8}$ x $5\frac{1}{2}$in (13 x 14cm) for top. For lining cut two pieces of fabric A: one measuring $6\frac{3}{4}$ x $18\frac{3}{4}$in (17 x 48cm); the other, $5\frac{1}{8}$ x $5\frac{1}{2}$ (13 x 14cm).

3 Stitch side to top. At each corner, pivot needle at pin position to form box shaping. On reaching starting point again, stitch over turned-back edge. Repeat steps 2 and 3 with pieces of fabric A, for the lining. Trim all seams.

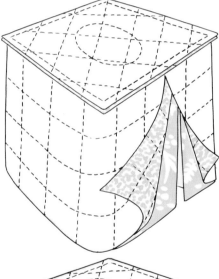

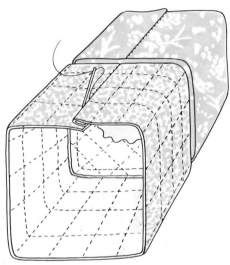

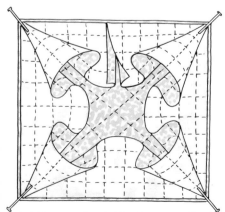

2 Join long quilted side piece to quilted top piece, as follows: place the top piece right side up on the work surface, and pin and baste the long piece to it, right sides together and raw edges even, starting in the middle of one side, with the beginning edge turned back $\frac{3}{8}$in (1cm). Keep a pin in each corner.

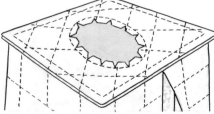

4 With right sides together, and tops matching at corners, pin the two layers together. Use the perforated center of a pop-up tissue box as your pattern. Place it centrally on the fabric top, as on the tissue box top. Draw around it to mark the hole position. Stitch just outside this line. Cut out oval along drawn line and discard. Clip curves very carefully to stitching.

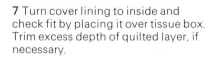

6 Pull the two layers apart, right sides out, as shown, and close the side edges with slip stitching.

7 Turn cover lining to inside and check fit by placing it over tissue box. Trim excess depth of quilted layer, if necessary.

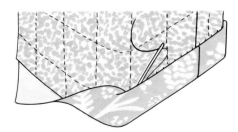

8 Bring bottom raw edge of lining to outside over quilted raw edge; turn under raw edge by $\frac{1}{4}$in (5mm), and slip stitch into position by hand on the outside forming a contrasting edge.

Terry Evans

Homemaker

Sheer Elegance

Light and elegant—these lovely draperies demonstrate what sheer fabrics can do for a window. An amazing variety of effects can be created with sheers, used on their own or along with curtains, shades and shutters.

Sheer fabrics are used in many different window treatments. Perhaps the most familiar kind of sheer window covering is glass curtains – plain full-length curtains made of smoothly woven fabric such as marquisette which are used along with panel or draw draperies to soften the light or give extra privacy. Plain sheer fabrics are also used for ruffled tie-backs – a style most often used in bedrooms.

Sheer fabrics with interesting textures are used on their own as draperies. They are particularly well suited to a modern room with picture windows or an entire wall of glass and can be a dramatic feature of the room, diffusing the light in interesting patterns and – in the case of colored fabrics – bathing the room in radiant color. Hung on a traverse rod, they can easily be opened.

Traditional-style windows can also be enhanced with sheer draperies. The variety of fabrics available includes styles that harmonize with period furnishings and some that complement them. You should have no trouble finding one suited to your decorating scheme.

Obviously sheers can only be used on their own if the window is in a secluded area or if full privacy is not required. If you need to be able to cover the window completely, a shade or shutters may be combined with sheer draperies in a way that is attractive as well as functional. Decorating books are full of ingenious combinations of different window coverings which you can copy or adapt to suit yourself. An attractive use of bamboo shades with sheer café curtains appears in a future Homemaker chapter. You can also use sheer draperies over glass curtains to create a fascinating interplay of textures.

Here we describe the fabrics suitable for both glass curtains and sheer draperies and the techniques you need to know to make them.

Fabrics

Fabrics suitable for glass curtains are generally made of polyester, nylon or fiberglass and are resistant to shrinking and fading. White is the most popular color, but cream, beige and some pastels are also used. You can, of course, buy ready-made glass curtains, but if you need curtains of an unusual length, or want color curtains instead of white or a finer fabric than is available in ready-made ones, then making them yourself is the answer.

Sheers suitable for draw draperies come in an amazing variety of styles, from nubby, coarsely woven types to delicately patterned traditional styles. Most are made of acrylic fibers, sometimes blended with wool, cotton or other synthetics.

Stitching sheer fabrics

Sheer curtains and draperies should always have double hems so that the cut edge of the fabric is not visible. Baste the hems carefully before stitching, as they are likely to slip if the fabric is synthetic. If the fabric is very slippery or has a particularly open weave, place strips of tissue paper above and below the two layers of fabric before stitching and tear the tissue away afterward. A roller presser foot is ideal for sewing lace fabrics because it will not snag.

Hems can be stitched by hand or by machine, using a fine needle and a sewing thread appropriate to the fabric. When stitching by machine, use long stitches and loosen the tension slightly to prevent pulling. And remember to make sure that your needle is sharp.

Joining fabric widths

Fine glass curtains will generally hang better if the widths are not joined. Each panel can be hung separately and the selvages left unhemmed, if they are neat.

Sheer fabrics are available in a wide variety of colors and textures – here we show a selection of lacy weaves and open weaves.

If you need to join widths of a fine fabric use either a small French seam or an interlocking fell seam, as shown in the instructions for making draperies on the next page. On heavier fabrics like cotton lace, you can use an ordinary flat seam. Press the seams open. If the selvages pull, snip them at intervals on both seam allowances. Alternatively, before sewing the widths together, cut the selvages off completely. This will prevent the edges from pulling.

If you are using a fabric in which woven areas alternate with open areas of loose threads (such as the rust-colored fabric in the photograph below), position your seams so that you stitch only through woven areas.

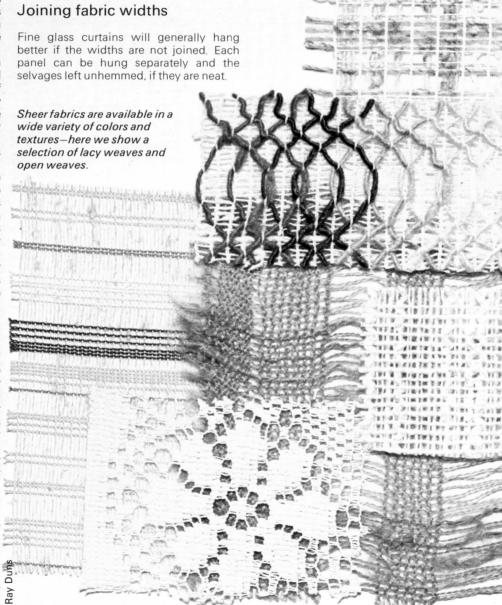

Ray Duns

121

Making glass curtains

Glass curtains are hung from a stationary adjustable curtain rod fixed next to the window, inside the drapery rod, if any. They are made with a casing, which slips over the rod and which may be either plain or headed.
For curtains which should not hang loose, make a casing on the bottom edge also.

Making sheer draperies

Sheer draperies are unlined and are usually made with a pinch-pleated heading. This is most easily made by using pleater tape, which contains pockets into which pronged hooks are inserted, to form the pleats. The most common type produces draperies of double fullness. The kind of tape you use will dictate the amount of fabric required, so choose the tape before buying the fabric. The amount of tape you need will, in turn, depend on the length of the drapery rod. So you must decide on the area you want the curtains to cover and then buy a rod of the appropriate type and length.

1 To figure the total width of fabric required for each window, first take the length of the rod, then add to this figure the fullness allowance for the tape you are using—that is, the amount taken up in pleats. This should be stated by the manufacturer.
If you are using a traditional-style pole with free-sliding rings (like the one shown on page 120), you can then simply add 2in (5cm) for each side hem and this will give you the width required. If, however, you are using a traverse rod, you will need to add the "return" at each outer edge. This is the part of the drapery from the corner of the rod to the wall; it covers the cords and the edges of any other window covering, such as a shade or glass curtains. The return will vary according to the rod's distance from the wall. In addition, if using a two-way draw traverse rod you will need to allow a little extra for the overlap at the center. Measure from the edge of the master slide, at the center, to the corner (where the outer pleat will be placed), then add the fullness allowance, the side hem allowances and the return. This is the width required for one panel. Double this figure for the amount required for both panels. Finally, divide the total width required by the width of your fabric, and round up the result to the nearest whole number (e.g. from 4.65 to 5) to get the number of fabric widths required. (If by chance the result should already be a whole

number, you will need to add a width to provide for seams.)
2 Figuring the length is much easier. Simply take the desired finished length and add to it the depth of the tape and 8in (20cm) for the bottom hem. Multiply this unfinished length by the number of fabric widths required, which will give you the amount of fabric required for the window. (Sheers rarely have patterns that need to be matched, but if yours does, you must buy extra, following the guidelines already given in Volume 1, page 114).
3 Cut the lengths to the measurement obtained in step 2 and join the fabric widths with flat seams, French seams or interlocking fell seams (see below), allowing $\frac{5}{8}$in (1.5cm) on each edge. If the fabric is loosely woven and apt to sag you should clip the selvages first.

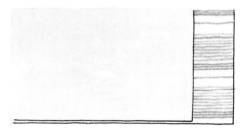

For an interlocking fell seam, lay the two pieces to be joined with right sides together and with the edge of the bottom layer extending $\frac{1}{4}$in (6mm) down the length of the seam.

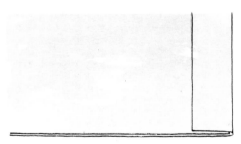

Turn the edge back over the top layer of fabric.

Fold both layers once more to form a seam $\frac{1}{4}$in (6mm) wide. Stitch close to the inside fold. This gives a neatened seam, with no stitching showing on the right side.
4 Cut excess width from the joined panels (use the cut width at the side of the panel). Turn 1in (2.5cm) to the wrong side along both sides of the

drapery. Fold again to form a 1in (2.5cm) double hem. Baste and stitch the double hem in place by hand or machine.

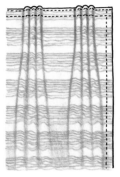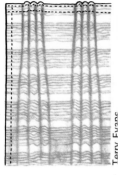

5 At the upper edge turn under a hem the same depth as the tape; press. Baste the tape over the folded edge, placing the pocket side upward and making sure that the slots in which the prongs are inserted are at the lower edge. The upper edge of the tape should be just below the fold and the ends of the tape should extend about $1\frac{1}{2}$in (4cm) past the hemmed edges of the drapery. Also, make sure to position the pockets so that you can form the first side pleat in the desired position; in the case of draperies with a return, the first prong should be inserted the return distance from the edge.
6 Trim the tape ends to about $\frac{1}{2}$in (1.2cm), fold them under and baste them in place. Machine stitch along all four sides of the tape close to the edges.
7 Turn up 4in (10cm) double hems at the lower edge and pin in place. Hang up the draperies and let them hang unhemmed for several days to allow the fabric to drop.
8 Make any necessary adjustments to the length—the draperies should clear the floor by about $\frac{1}{2}$in (1.2cm). Take them down. Trim the hem allowance to an even depth. Turn up half the hem allowance, then the other half. Pin and baste the hem in place. Machine-stitch the hem or hem it by hand.

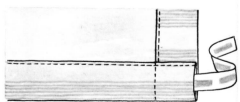

9 To help the draperies hang evenly insert a length of lightweight weighted tape into the hems. Secure the tape at the outside edges with a few stitches. Remove it before cleaning the draperies.
10 Finally, slip stitch the edges together at the sides of each hem.

Curtains with a plain casing

1 Measure the width and length of the window area the curtains will cover. Multiply the width by 2½ or 3 and add 2in (5cm) for each side hem required. To the finished curtain length add between 8 and 10in (20 to 25cm) for the bottom hem and 3¼in (8cm) for the top casing. Full-length glass curtains should clear the floor by about ½in (1.2cm).
2 To estimate the amount of fabric required for each window, divide the unhemmed width of both panels by the width of your chosen fabric, which will give you the number of fabric widths required, then multiply this number by the unhemmed length of the curtains.
3 Cut the fabric into lengths according to the measurements obtained in step 1. If you are joining widths to make two panels you may need to cut one length in half lengthwise in order to make up the correct width for each panel. Join the fabric lengths, if you like, using French seams.
4 On the side edges (and the center edges if you are making two panels) turn under and stitch double 1in (2.5cm) hems.

5 Turn 1⅝in (4cm) to the wrong side at the top edge of the curtain. Fold over the top again to make a 1⅝in (4cm)-wide double hem. Press and machine-stitch close to the lower fold so that you form a casing. (Check the casing over the curtain rod to make sure it can be accommodated easily.)
6 Turn up the curtains to the correct length and pin a double hem in place at the lower edge. Try the curtain on the rod to check the length. Adjust then machine-stitch the hem in place.
7 Insert a length of weighted tape in the hem and secure it with a few stitches at the side edge.

Curtains with a headed casing

These are made in much the same way as curtains with a plain casing.
1 Estimate the total fabric width required in the same way as for plain headed curtains. Add between 8 and 10in (20 and 25cm) for the bottom hem to the finished length of the curtain. Allow twice the depth of the heading plus 3¼in (8cm) for the casing itself. The longer the drop of the curtain, the deeper the heading may be, up to a depth of about 1½in (4cm).
2 Join fabric widths, if necessary. Turn under and stitch double side hems.

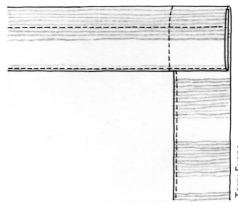

Terry Evans

3 Fold half the allowance (including the casing allowance) at the top of the curtain to the wrong side. Fold again and stitch in place close to the bottom fold. Add another line of stitching 1 to 1¼in (2.5 to 3cm) above the first line.
4 Turn up double hems at the bottom and pin in place. Hang up and check the length, adjust and stitch in place.
5 Insert weighted tape in the hems, as for "Curtains with a plain casing."

Note If you are making curtains with casings at top and bottom—for example, for French doors—be sure to check the length carefully before you stitch the casings in place, so that the curtains cover the area smoothly, neither pulling nor drooping between the rods.

Camera Press

Needlework

Materials
¾yd (.7m) medium-weight unbleached
   muslin 36in (90cm) wide
⅛yd (.1m) each of 4 contrasting
   cotton fabrics 36in (90cm) wide
Felt—orange, turquoise, pink, red,
   dark green—4in (10cm) square;
   light green—12in (30cm) square;
   scraps of white and black felt
White sewing thread
Black and white stranded cotton
   embroidery floss
6in (15cm) white zipper
3 medium-sized snap fasteners
1in (2.5cm) green button
1 white shoelace, 18in (45cm) long
8 white eyelets and punch (optional)
Tracing paper and dressmaker's carbon

One, two, buckle my shoe . . .

Learning how to get dressed is child's play with the help of this appealing rag book. A bright red felt shoe and a happy frog will help your child master zippers and shoelaces; a button-down pocket and snap-on flower petals will also teach and entertain at the same time.

Kim Sayer

124

1 First wash the muslin, as this fabric will probably shrink quite a lot. Iron it while it is still damp to remove creases.

2 Trace all pattern pieces on the tracing paper. Cut out each piece on the appropriate fabric. Large, simple shapes can be pinned to the fabric and cut around. Smaller pieces and those with intricate shapes should be traced on the fabric using dressmaker's carbon paper. Place the carbon between the fabric and the tracing paper and firmly trace the outline with a pencil or ballpoint pen. Cut out the shapes.

3 Cut the muslin into 6 pieces, each measuring approximately 14in (35cm) by 12in (30cm).

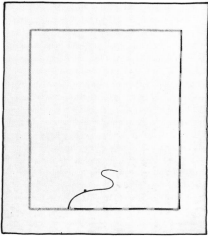

4 In the center of each piece of muslin, measure and draw a rectangle 12in (30cm) by 8½in (22cm). Baste along this outline.

Cover page

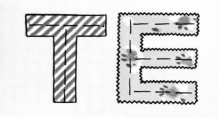

1 Place the letters, flower pieces and leaf stem in position within the basted lines on one of the muslin pages. When you are satisfied that the lettering is well spaced and straight, pin and baste all the pieces in place. Set your sewing machine to a narrow zig-zag stitch, and —using white thread—stitch around all the letters and leaves. Alternatively, hand sew the shapes to the page, using blanket stitch (see Volume 2, page 62). Make sure the raw edges are covered by the line of stitching, as this not only attaches the pieces to the muslin but also prevents the appliquéd pieces from fraying.

2 Draw all loose ends through to the wrong side and tie securely. Remove all basting threads. Do not, however, remove the basting lines around the pages at this stage.

Page 1—frog and zipper

1 Pin, baste, and zig-zag stitch the grass in place on a muslin page. Pin and baste the zipper in place under the frog's mouth slit. Using the zipper foot of the machine and a straight stitch, carefully stitch all around mouth, close to edges, to secure the zipper in place.

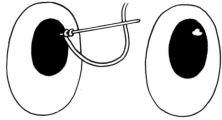

2 Using six strands of black embroidery floss, work two French knots (see Volume 4, page 113) to form the nostrils. Hand sew the black pupils to the white eye pieces, and then work two French knots in white stranded embroidery floss to make a "twinkle" in each eye. Pin and baste the eyes in place on the frog.

3 Pin and baste the frog in place on the muslin page and zig-zag stitch around all raw edges. Also stitch around the eyes and around the body shape, using the dashed line on the pattern as a guide. Remove basting threads and tie loose ends.

Page 2—flowers and snap fasteners

1 Place the leaf stems in position on a muslin page as shown on page 128. Pin and baste. Zig-zag stitch in place.

2 Pin and baste the centers of the flowers in place on the felt shapes. Zig-zag stitch around the raw edges of centers and tie ends off neatly.

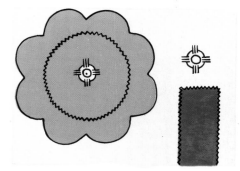

3 In the center of the wrong side of each flower, hand sew one part of a snap; make sure you do not stitch through to the right side of the flower centers. Arrange the flower heads above each stalk, and lightly mark on the muslin the position of the snaps. Sew the other parts of the snaps in place. Remove basting threads and tie ends.

Terry Evans

LETTERS

FLOWER PETALS

FLOWER CENTER

LEAF STEM

FROG

EYE

PUPIL

GRASS

PUPIL
cut 2 black felt

EYE
cut 2 white felt

FROG
cut 1 light green felt

cut 1 printed cotton

cut 2 printed cotton

cut slit for zipper mouth

cut 1 light green felt

cut 1 printed cotton

line of stitching

FLOWER PETALS
cut 1 cotton

cut 1 printed cotton

cut 1 printed cotton

FLOWER CENTER
cut 1 cotton

GRASS
cut 1 dark green felt

LEAF STEM
cut 1 dark green felt

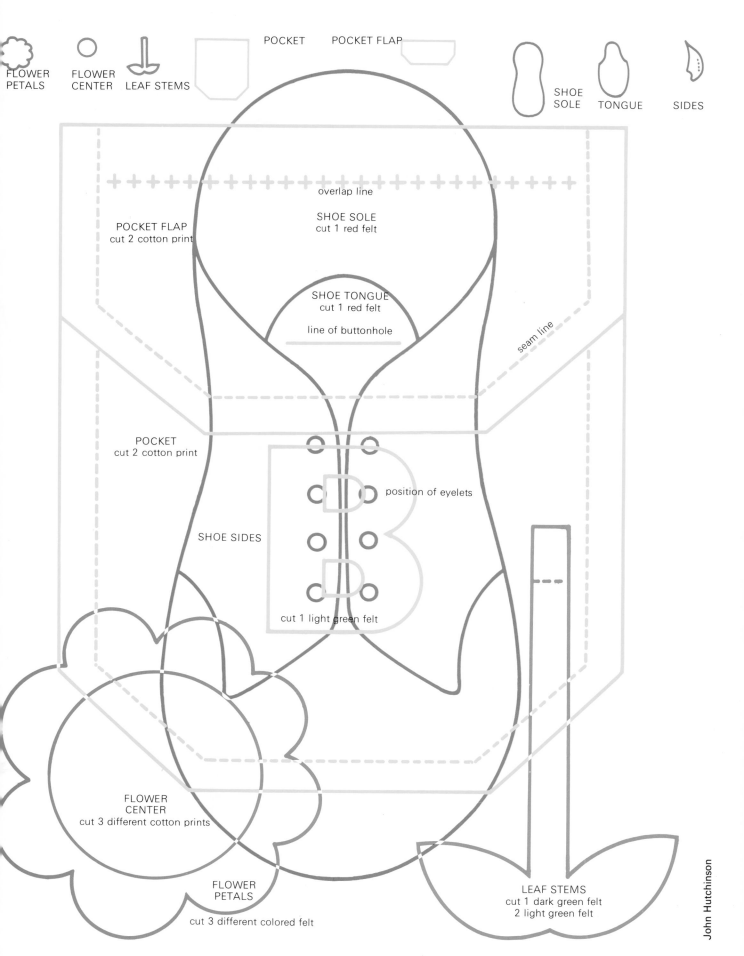

FLOWER
PETALS

FLOWER
CENTER

LEAF STEMS

POCKET

POCKET FLAP

SHOE
SOLE

TONGUE

SIDES

overlap line

POCKET FLAP
cut 2 cotton print

SHOE SOLE
cut 1 red felt

SHOE TONGUE
cut 1 red felt

line of buttonhole

seam line

POCKET
cut 2 cotton print

position of eyelets

SHOE SIDES

cut 1 light green felt

FLOWER
CENTER
cut 3 different cotton prints

FLOWER
PETALS

cut 3 different colored felt

LEAF STEMS
cut 1 dark green felt
2 light green felt

John Hutchinson

Page 3—pocket and button

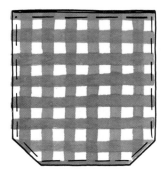

1 Pin and baste the two pocket pieces together, right sides facing; repeat for pocket flap pieces. Machine-stitch along seamlines of pocket and flap, leaving gaps of 2in (5cm) along top edges. Turn both sections right side out. Baste around all the edges, including the 2in (5cm) gap which was left unstitched. Press both sections.

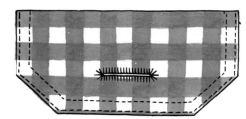

2 On the pocket piece pin and baste the letter ''B''; zig-zag stitch along edges. On the flap, work a buttonhole—either by machine or by hand—to fit the green button. Straight stitch around lower and side edges of flap, close to the edge. Add a second line of stitching about ¼in (5mm) inside the first line. Repeat on upper edge of pocket.

3 Center the pocket on a muslin page; pin and baste. Using straight stitch, secure the pocket in place with two lines of stitching along the sides and base. Place the pocket flap slightly above the pocket and straight stitch

along top of flap with two lines of stitching. Hand sew the button to the pocket underneath the buttonhole.

Page 4—shoe and laces

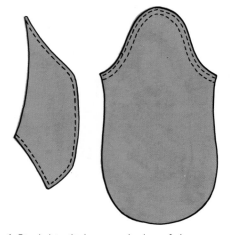

1 Straight stitch around edge of shoe side pieces, except for outer edges. Also stitch twice around the upper edge of the tongue, placing the two lines of stitching close to each other.

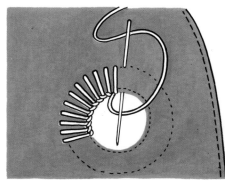

2 If you have an eyelet punch, use it to make four eyelets on each of the side pieces to take the shoelace. Or make the eyelets by hand, using two strands of white embroidery floss and close blanket stitch.

3 Pin pieces of shoe on sole, then position shoe on muslin page; pin, baste and straight stitch a double line around the shoe edge. Insert shoelace.

Putting the book together

1 Press each page on the wrong side. Pin and baste the cover page and page 1 together. Similarly, join pages 2 and 3, page 4 and the blank page. Remember to match up the original basted lines. Straight stitch inside the new basting lines, ¼in (5mm) from the original basting line around each page. Trim with pinking shears.

2 Put the pages on top of one another in the correct order. Pin along left side and then straight stitch close to the edge several times in the same place to hold the pages together securely. Remove all remaining basting threads.

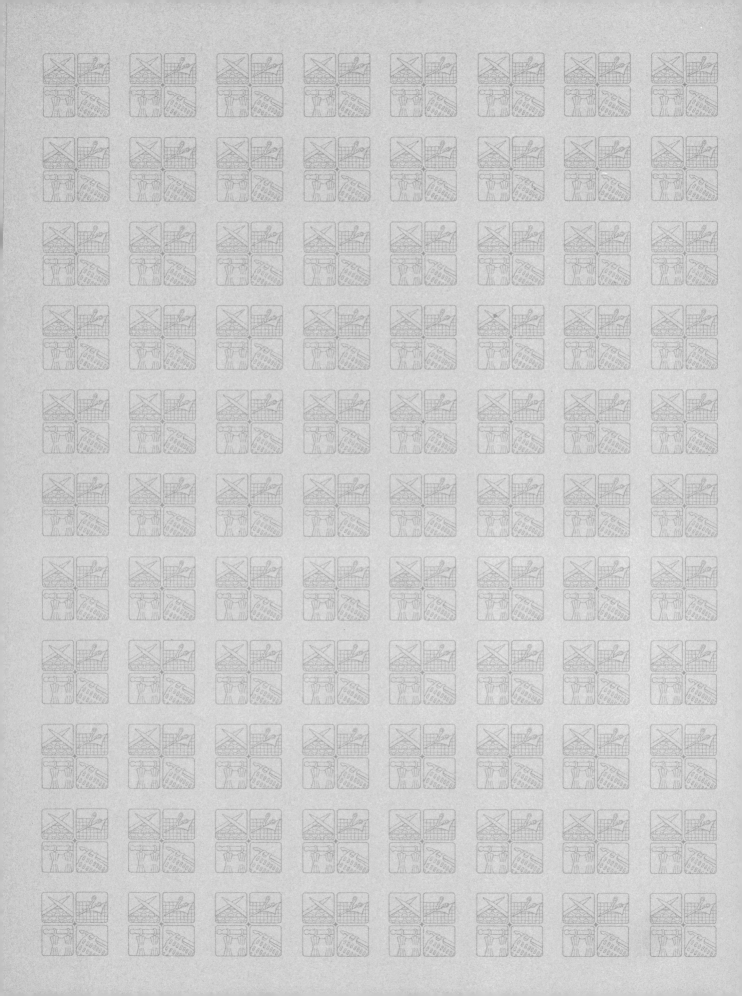